To John and Dorothy Fimister
with thanks for everything.

Acknowledgements

Firstly, thanks are due to my partner and to my daughter, Anne and Katie, for their forbearance as I have disappeared into my study at every available opportunity over the last several months in order to complete this book. To my son Alan, moreover, is owed a debt of gratitude more directly related to the completion of the task: in order to produce this work fully up-to-date and on schedule, it was necessary for me to make the long-over-due transition from typewriter to computer, a metamorphosis which would have been far more difficult without his technical guidance.

As regards the contents of these pages, while the responsibility is of course mine, I owe much to the very helpful, perceptive and expert observations of those friends and colleagues who read and commented upon drafts. My very great thanks, therefore, are due to Lynda Bransbury, Ann Davis, Michael Hill, Bob Hudson, Guy Robertson, Pauline Thompson, Gary Vaux and Nick Whitton. I am most grateful, also, to Brian Roycroft for contributing the foreword. I hope the results justify their generous support.

Geoff Fimister
Newcastle upon Tyne
April 1995

Business Education Publishers Limited
1995

32-55 61   101

© Geoff Fimister

ISBN 0 907679 82 X

First published September 1995

Published in Great Britain by Business Education Publishers Limited
Leighton House 10 Grange Crescent Stockton Road
Sunderland Tyne & Wear SR2 7BN

Tel. 0191 567 4963 Fax. 0191 514 3277

British Cataloguing-in-Publications Data
A catalogue record for this book is available from the British Library

Printed in Great Britain by Athenaeum Press - Newcastle

The Author

Geoff Fimister originates from Liverpool and undertook research in various areas of social policy at Loughborough and Glasgow Universities before moving to Newcastle upon Tyne in 1974 to set up Newcastle City Council's Welfare Rights Service. He has continued to work in Newcastle, where he is a Principal Welfare Rights Officer, since that time. He has for many years been a Welfare Rights Adviser to the Association of Metropolitan Authorities, working on the benefit aspects of a range of social services, housing and financial issues. He is regularly involved in consultations with central government and in Parliamentary lobbying and has been a member of the AMA teams working on housing benefit and on community care throughout the changes in both of those fields during the 1980s and 1990s. He has undertaken similar advisory work for, amongst others, the Association of Directors of Social Services and the European Economic and Social Committee. He has been a member of the National Executive Committee of the Child Poverty Action Group since 1979. He has written and lectured extensively on social security and welfare rights issues.

Foreword

Let me quote to you an extract from the Day Book of the Master of the Poor Law Institution in Newcastle, for 4th. December, 1884:

"Numbers present at 6 am - 51 of whom 23 were male and 17 were children. Numbers present at 5 pm when the doors were closed - 55. Four were discharged during the day. Two males had died from old age and the phlegm. One child discharged to hospital unlikely to return. Emily Hankinson died. Admitted during the day eight people. Emily Millburn with three children following the death of her husband who was a Keelman. She is entitled to a Keelman's pension of one shilling and four pence and two pence for each child per week. This will be paid by the Borough. Admitted one vagrant who will be sent to South Shields. Admitted one Miner with a broken arm. He will not work again. Mr. George Armstrong of The Manor, South Gosforth, kindly brought a waif across the saddle of his horse. The waif had been found on the drive leading to his house. On stripping and washing the waif was discovered to be female. Pointed out to Mr. Armstrong that his house was outside the boundaries of the Borough, and he left one shilling for the care of the waif. The waif died before nightfall. Will return sevenpence to Mr. Armstrong in balance".

Over a century later, things have changed - but have they changed enough? The aspirations of community care are noble: to enable as many elderly, ill or disabled people as possible to live a fulfilling life outside of institutions; and when residential care is necessary, to ensure that it is of a high standard. Our approach to the wellbeing of children has also come a long way since 1884. But there are still many problems. Our services may have noble aims, but they are seriously under-financed. Poverty has not been banished and - in its modern forms - is indeed on the advance. The benefit system today is greatly superior to anything known to Emily Millburn, although it still fails to prevent poverty, is under hostile scrutiny by a Government in search of savings and interacts with our care services in ways far more complex and problematic than did Mrs. Millburn's Keelman's pension.

This book is about community care, the benefit system, the complicated relationships between them and the implications for service users, carers, advisers, local authorities and other agencies and individuals. I can think of nobody better qualified to write it than Geoff Fimister. I worked with him for nearly 20 years during my time as Director of Social Services in

Newcastle and watched him build up the Welfare Rights Service from a one-person band to the impressive network of advice, advocacy, training, information, publicity and policy services which it became.

In the 1980s and 1990s, the almost annual task of steering a course for the Welfare Rights Service through the rocks of Government-imposed spending cuts was added to Geoff's duties, but throughout all this, we never lost sight of the need to pursue the policy issues, as well as keep services afloat. From the outset, Geoff has made available his advisory and lobbying skills to the Association of Metropolitan Authorities - and I could fill several large boxes with the briefings which he wrote for me during my time as Honorary Secretary of the Association of Directors of Social Services. There was also the international dimension: as a Member of the European Economic and Social Committee in the mid-1980s, I worked with Geoff on several projects around social security and anti-poverty issues.

Social security in relation to community care has for some years been one of Geoff Fimister's particular interests. This has been reflected in his work with the Local Authority Associations, which has involved him in the thick of the consultations with central government which led up to - and have continued beyond - the introduction in 1993 of the new system of community care organisation and funding. In this book, he brings together an analysis of the policies, a description of the structures and processes and an eye for the background politics, in those crucial areas where the community care and benefit systems overlap. I am very happy to commend it to the reader.

Brian Roycroft CBE
April 1995

Preface

The worlds of health care and community care have been revolutionised by the 1990 NHS and Community Care Act. Organisations have been split into purchasing and providing arms, attempts have been made to fuse the market ethic with traditional welfare values, structures and funding have been fundamentally altered, new measures to monitor performance and assure quality have been introduced, and a more prominent role for users and carers has been promised. These measures affect policy-makers, managers, front-line staff and users alike.

Although the main legislation was passed in 1990, it is only now that some of the practical dilemmas surrounding the implementation of such professional, organisational and cultural change are being confronted. This series seeks to provide an informed commentary upon the changes. The first two volumes were published in 1994. Bob Hudson took an overview of the role of markets in both health and community care, while Andrew Nocon explored the issue of collaboration between health and community care agencies. This third volume by Geoff Fimister examines the critical area of social security and community care. In a way, social security has been the joker in the community care pack - ostensibly a side show in the wider pursuit of a more user-sensitive approach, but in reality the raison d'etre of the White Paper both in terms of reducing expenditure on private care and refocusing the cash-care boundary. Geoff Fimister has long experience of the role of social security in community care, both in terms of the practicalities of specific benefits and the issues behind policy formulation and implementation. It is this blend of policy and practice which makes 'Social Security and Community Care in the 1990s' such an important contribution to this series. Although sophisticated in approach, the author does not assume previous knowledge. He looks at the historical experience and the current benefit structure, as well as some emerging issues. I believe this volume fills a much needed niche in the literature on community care.

Bob Hudson,
Series Editor.

Table of Contents

Chapter 1

Introduction

In April 1993, local authority (LA) Social Services Departments (SSDs) acquired the lead responsibility for the finance and co-ordination of "care in the community" for elderly people and those of any age with physical and mental illness or disability of one kind or another. (Although this book is focused on the position in England and Wales, the term "SSD" can usually also be taken to reflect the situation in Scottish Social Work Departments, where the issues are generally, although not invariably, similar. Readers interested in the position in Northern Ireland will also recognise many familiar issues in these pages, although the governmental structure there is very different at local level. For a note on the sense in which the phrases "care in the community" and "community care" are used in this book, see appendix 3).

The intensive activity which has surrounded, over the last few years, the planning and implementation of the new system has had many positive outcomes, as a much higher profile has been given to the needs of service users and carers. There is no doubt that a higher quality of life has been achieved for some vulnerable people than would otherwise have been the case. For others, though, quality of life has been adversely affected, as under-financing has led to service reductions and new or increased charges.

Undoubtedly one of the most controversial aspects of under-resourcing has been the closure of hospitals for people who are mentally ill, without the provision of adequate community-based alternatives. In the Summer of 1993, a few months after the launch of the new community care arrangements, I visited London in the company of my teenage son. (He was on holiday and I was in town for a meeting with the Department of Health (DoH) and the Department of Social Security (DSS)). As we sauntered one evening along Islington's trendy Upper Street, we approached a shop doorway which I knew from experience was often inhabited by a man who was mentally ill. As we drew near, the man suddenly emitted a loud moan, rolled onto his side and across the pavement into the gutter. He then moaned again and - like a film running in reverse

- rolled back across the pavement and resumed his original position. "Look, Dad", said my son, "community care!"

By no means all of the homeless people sleeping and/ or begging in London's shop doorways and railway concourses are mentally ill. But many are. In a letter to the Guardian newspaper later in 1983, the secretary and chair of an organisation called Concern reported that: "We have found that 20 per cent of the destitute interviewed in London had active hallucinations and one in eight had never received any psychiatric care. A further 20 per cent had received psychiatric in-patient care for psychosis, but were now sleeping rough. Over a third were not receiving any benefits at all". (Hollander and Weller 1993).

Such problems, though particularly acute in London, are by no means confined to the capital. Is it perhaps a matter of "client group"? That is, do homeless mentally ill people receive a lower priority than categories of client who are perceived as more "deserving"? There may well be something in this hypothesis, but on the other hand, there is no doubt that a shortfall in resources for community care can and does affect various client groups to varying degrees in different parts of the country, as an inadequate cake is cut up in an eccentric way. As I put the final touches to the text of this book (April 1995) public and political controversy over funding shortfalls, high charges and inadequate services for elderly and disabled people is growing by the week. More of this in later chapters.

However, this book is not primarily about an overview of the community care changes, or of their general financial structure. Rather, we are concerned here with the social security aspects of community care - an area at once crucial and often highly confusing.

Social security is important to community care for a number of reasons. For elderly or disabled people seeking to remain in their own homes, or perhaps in some form of supported accommodation falling short of full residential care, the level of disposable income may make the crucial difference, determining how far a person is able to afford a suitable diet, sufficient clothing, adequate warmth, appropriate housing and participation in social activities.

Similar factors apply when a person living in a residential or hospital setting wishes to be resettled in the wider community. As I have argued elsewhere (e.g. Fimister, 1988) it seems as though, the further towards a position of independence a person is able to travel, the stronger are the forces threatening to push him or her back again in the other direction. For example, as long as a former patient with mental health problems is not well enough to "sign on" as available for work, he or she will be able to claim earnings- replacement benefits and additional means-tested benefits which will be much higher than those available to a claimant who is required to register for employment. Thus, when our ex-patient recovers sufficiently to be able to sign on, he or she will sustain a severe cut in income, as policies relating to labour discipline are activated and override community care considerations. (For example, loss of the income support disability premium, as a result of signing on, is an income cut of 19-80 per week at 1995/6 rates).

Similarly, a former patient newly out of hospital may be able to obtain a "community care grant" from the Social Fund to pay for essential items of furniture or household equipment; but thereafter is likely to be offered a loan at best, being pushed deeper into poverty by the subsequent repayments. In hospital or a residential care home, a long-stay resident will not have to pay council tax: but outside, liability to pay and draconian penalties for default will have to be coped with. For all these reasons and more, information, advice and advocacy to maximise income and deal with benefit problems will very frequently make an essential difference to survival chances in that often deceptively cosy-sounding place, "the community". (See also Betteridge and Davis, 1990, and Davis, Flynn and Murray, 1993, for further illustration of how the social security system, structurally and administratively, can work against community care objectives).

It is not only elderly, ill and disabled people who should be our focus of interest in terms of social security and community care. There is also the question of the very large numbers of informal carers: those who look after their vulnerable relatives and friends and without whose efforts the system simply could not function in anything like its present form. As the Government's community care White Paper recognised: "the reality is that most care is provided by family, friends or neighbours".(DoH, 1989, para. 2.3).

Carers are themselves frequently elderly and vulnerable. They are also frequently poor, but - although they are often praised by government - "Frankly… weighed against the other priorities within the budget, we are giving as much help to carers as we can manage at the moment". (Minister for the Disabled Nicholas Scott, in evidence to the House of Commons Social Services Committee (1990b, para. 73)).

Commenting on Richard Titmuss's fear that "community care" might be a rhetorical smoke-screen for a lack of adequate provision for people such as those who are mentally ill (Titmuss, 1963, p104), Sally Baldwin observes that: "A later generation of feminist policy analysts has added to this a concern with the implications..... for informal carers, predominantly women. At present levels of support..... community care policies signal a major increase in the responsibilities carried by informal carers - with all that implies for their quality of life. On this analysis community care policies can increase the capacity of many people with disabilities to lead "ordinary lives" only by diminishing the capacity of their carers to do so". (Baldwin, 1988, p3). This phenomenon is well-illustrated in Caroline Glendinning's in-depth study of working-age carers (Glendinning, 1992) which also highlights the destructive effect on savings and pension rights which caring can entail - that is, the carer is all too often building up poverty for his or her old age. (See also Hancock and Jarvis, 1994, who report similar findings; and Scope, 1995, for an account of many carers' perceptions of their own situations). These are sobering reminders that informal carers must have their own place in our deliberations on the social security aspects of community care.

We should also remember that, if service users and carers often face daunting obstacles in seeking to keep going and achieve an acceptable quality of life, then such challenges are all the greater for those whose status as care recipient or carer is overlaid by some other form of discrimination or disadvantage. Obviously, this is very much the case where the person concerned is a member of an ethnic minority community who may experience language difficulties, cultural misunderstandings or overt racism in his or her dealings with public bureaucracies, not least in relation to the securing of social security entitlements. Increasingly, bodies such as the Benefits Agency and the more progressive LAs pursue "good practice" objectives in such matters, but racism - whether structural or individual, subconscious or overt - is deeply ingrained in our society and there is a very long way to go. (See Divine and Vaux, 1988; and Deacon, Hylton, Karmani and Law, 1994, regarding the obstacles to claiming which people from ethnic minority communities experience).

Another important dimension of the relationship between social security and community care concerns the links between benefits and the funding mechanisms of the new system. As we shall see in chapters 2 and 3, most of the benefits which care home residents claim go towards the cost of their care; the transfer of funds from the DSS to SSDs which launched the new system was based on a benefit-related formula; and increasingly, service users living in their own homes are finding that their benefits are taken into account in determining charges. There is, moreover, a substantial overlap between benefit matters and many issues around housing and community care, such as affordability of rents and the finance of various forms of supported accommodation.

Given these numerous aspects of the subject, it would be as well to set out clearly what this book is and is not intended to do.

What is this Book for?

The Association of Metropolitan Authorities (AMA) and Association of County Councils (ACC) have a joint Welfare Rights Advisers' Group, consisting of about half a dozen specialists from each association, charged with advising these bodies and assisting with consultations with central government. A division of labour operates and I am one of several advisers who have a particular role in relation to community care matters. As well as providing briefings and being involved in consultations and Parliamentary lobbying, this role includes fielding enquiries from all over Britain on issues relating to social security and community care. This has given me a good idea of what elements of the system are causing the most confusion "on the ground". Queries come from local authority and health service staff engaged in planning and delivering services; from elected councillors; from academics, voluntary organisations and the media; and from service users and carers. As the new system settles down, it steadily becomes easier for answers to be found locally, without needing to consult LA Association advisers: but to the extent that the position remains uncertain and fluid, enquiries continue to flow in. This can be difficult to handle operationally, but is a most valuable source of feedback, as are the numerous briefing sessions and seminars which one is asked to provide.

So what are the Problems?

Social security as it relates to community care represents one of the most difficult aspects of a difficult system. If we look at benefit provisions overall, we can see that they are not only painfully complex, but also subject to a process of continuous change. At any given time, it is likely that one substantial upheaval or another is either under way or in the pipeline, or both; while batches of detailed amendment regulations arrive with alarming frequency. There are several reasons for this, tied up with the politics of public expenditure; the impact of other policy areas (employment, housing or local government taxation, for example); and the legal and technical difficulties which are inherent in a heavy reliance on means-testing.

One also suspects that there is a certain macho "complexity culture" pervading the drafting of benefit law. As an article in the Law Society Gazette put it (commenting on social security law in general, but giving an example from the community care field):"Cross-references - to sub-sections, to other sections, to schedules, to a myriad of regulations and indeed to other Acts -proliferate. One finds exceptions to exceptions to exceptions. Double and even triple negatives almost seem like a badge of honour: no self-respecting section is complete without one". (Thomas, 1993, p25). Or as Lord Justice Glidewell put it, in a case concerning the severe disability premium (a provision described in chapter 3): "...it is deplorable that legislation which affects some of the most disadvantaged people in society should be couched in language which is so difficult for even a lawyer trained and practising in this field to understand". (Bate v. Chief Adjudication Officer, Court of Appeal, 30.11.94). For our present purposes, suffice it to say that the grafting of the new community care arrangements onto this system has created a good deal of bafflement on the ground as to what benefits service users might be entitled to and what is the current state of play as the rules of entitlement continue to mutate.

Nor, it might be added, is such bafflement only to be found at "ground level". Senior civil servants in the relevant policy units and welfare rights advisers working with the LA Associations have spent many long hours arguing amongst themselves and with each other about what this or that aspect of the law actually means, is intended to mean or achieves in practice.

It is with *bafflement*, then, that this book is partly concerned. Insofar as it is possible - and I do not wish to promise the impossible! - I should like to try to shed some light on what is happening and why. This is not, though, a rights guide: it does not set out to provide a reference work which will explain detailed social security entitlements. The reader should indeed bear in mind that, except for historical material, technical details in the text reflect the position as it was in April 1995. Such is the rate of change that some of this is likely to have altered within a few months. (Something is said in chapter 3 about possible sources of detailed welfare rights information). Rather, this is an *issues* book: it deals with policies, their origins and purposes, the dilemmas surrounding them, and how they seem to be working out in reality.

We are also concerned in these pages with *planning blight*. Those who are trying to plan services and projects and who have to make assumptions about revenue from rents and charges to be paid by residents and service users have, especially over the last decade, been sorely tried by an ever-present background of rule changes - actual, projected or just rumoured - as well as by rules which, while not changing for the moment, are administered so variably that the outcome in any given case cannot readily be predicted. I cannot promise to clarify that which is literally ambiguous, nor to bring moving goal posts to a halt, but I may be able usefully to analyse some of the problems.

Another increasingly fluid factor is the political scene. The completion of this book is taking place at a time when the Government's position in the House of Commons has been weakened, through by-election setbacks and dissidence in the ranks, to the extent that important legislation is no longer assured of safe passage. The next General Election may be earlier than hitherto supposed and the outcome is difficult to foresee. Some speculation on the implications of different political agendas can be found in chapter 7.

In tackling the above, I shall try to remember that my readers will range from those who are welfare rights specialists to those who have only a broad knowledge of benefit rules. I shall therefore seek to avoid both the frequent use of legal references and the extreme reaches of technical complexity. I apologise to welfare rights technicality-junkies for this, but I am sure that it will be welcome to most readers - if I can achieve it! Chapter 3 includes a brief summary of the benefits which are most relevant within the community care context.

The use of *specialist terminology* also requires comment. The social security issues range across several professional, bureaucratic or otherwise specialised fields - benefits; local government; social work; service users' organisations - all with their own languages. Welfare rights advisers necessarily venture into all of these worlds, so if the terminology used in this book is sometimes hybrid, I hope nevertheless that its meaning and context will be clear. To supplement the summary of benefits contained in chapter 3, moreover, I have provided in appendix 3 a brief glossary of other specialised terms and the sense in which they are used. Other aids to comprehension are appendix 1 (a key to abbreviations used in the text) and appendix 2 (a chronology of key events from 1980 onwards).

A further point concerns *transitional arrangements* between the new and the old systems. With the important exception of inhabitants of private and voluntary sector residential care and nursing homes, I do not in general intend to delve into detailed transitional provisions: they tend to be highly technical and for most readers will not in any case be of continuing interest.

I believe that my involvement (both as Principal Welfare Rights Officer with Newcastle City Council and as an AMA adviser) in the changes with which we are concerned here, has its advantages and disadvantages as regards the writing of this book. There is much interesting research and practice which the operational realities of writing "on the hoof" have not left me time to explore to the extent to which I would have wished. On the other hand, I have been able to gather together a good deal of information from different parts of the country and can also offer an "insider's view" of much of the history and many of the policy debates.

Ultimately, if this book manages to interest and illuminate to at least some degree, while also perhaps helping some more money to flow to service users and carers, then it will have met its objectives.

Chapter 2

The History: how we got to where we are

Summary

This chapter traces the tangled history of the relationship between community care funding and the social security system, focusing particularly on the period since 1980, when changes to the benefit rules helped to stimulate a rapid growth in private sector residential care. Recognising the irony that community care policy has been substantially driven by the financial politics of residential care, changes in benefit rules relating to residential care and nursing homes are described, culminating in the transition, in April 1993, to a system in which lead responsibility for "gatekeeping", allocating and financing care services, both residential and non-residential, passed to local authority SSDs. The new benefit arrangements in relation to residential care and nursing homes are then briefly described (as a preliminary to a more detailed treatment in chapter 3) while the aspiration is noted that in future part of the resources transferred from the benefit system to SSDs as a result of the change would be used, where appropriate, to maintain people outside of residential care settings.

The narrative then backtracks to look at what has happened in recent years to "small homes", hostels, supported lodgings and similar "half-way" provision between residential care and fully independent living. The process is described whereby, here too, the DSS has substantially extricated itself from a funding role.

There are other relevant histories which, for reasons of space, cannot be described in detail here - notably, developments in retirement pensions and in disability benefits. These and other sets of benefits are, though, referred to throughout the book and are briefly described in chapter 3.

The Policy Background

To understand where we are now, it is first necessary to remind ourselves of how we got here. The history of the issues with which this book is concerned can be traced back a long way, arguably to the Elizabethan Poor Law. Certainly, the 1948 distinction between National Health Service (NHS) care (free at the point of access) and means-tested LA care, is of abiding importance. However, I would like to start the story more recently, around the time of the rapid growth of private and voluntary sector care home provision in the early 1980s.

This is a complex tale concerning not only the theory and practice of community care, but also the competing agendas of different government departments and other vested interests. The official version of course involves a rational decision-making process, whereby it was recognised that public finances could be better deployed and community care objectives more effectively pursued if resources were organised in a different way. As ever, the reality is more interesting. While there is undoubtedly to be found a "community care philosophy" within the Department of Health and amongst local authorities and voluntary organisations, many commentators (including this one) believe that it is upon the Department of Social Security (and the Treasury) that one must focus in order to identify the most important driving force behind the reforms. (Readers should note that the old Department of Health and Social Security (DHSS) was divided in 1988 into two distinct departments, although its two wings had in any case operated with a considerable degree of separation. Unless the context suggests otherwise, I shall refer to the "DoH" and "DSS" when considering events which span the reorganisation).

The DSS has, during the 1980s and 1990s, worked hard to divest itself of its responsibilities in the care field. The current range of disability-related benefits seems still to be considered by the Department to be a legitimate part of its functions, but other aspects of income rights which bear upon care matters have been seen as an unwelcome complication. Partly, this is a result of computerisation. The social security system has changed radically over the last decade in the degree to which computer technology is used in its administration. Much of the restructuring which has gone on has been designed to facilitate this, including the lopping off of difficult "messy bits" which did not lend themselves to such streamlining - for example, the abolition in 1988 of the "additional requirements" allowances, most of which related to disability, which were once available under the (then) supplementary benefit scheme. The intrusion of care considerations into benefit calculations was another such encumbrance, special rules for board and lodging and hostel accommodation - much of which provided care - being abolished in 1989 (see below).

Perhaps the major factor, though, was the escalating cost of benefit payments in respect of private and voluntary (P&V) sector residential care and nursing homes. In the local authority care home sector, the role of benefit payments, in any given case, was relatively minor. (Except, that is, for a temporary period from 1984-6, when it was accepted by the DHSS that - contrary to the Government's intentions - some residents of LA residential care homes could claim housing benefit (HB). This "loophole" was closed with effect from July 1986, although disputes between the Department and various LAs - sometimes in court - concerning the proper extent of entitlement during that period, dragged on for years afterwards). The minimum charge which LAs levied in their residential care homes was set at four fifths of the basic retirement pension, with one fifth remaining to the resident as a "personal expenses allowance". This meant that claimants only needed to have recourse to means-tested social assistance ("supplementary benefit" until 1988, when it was reconstituted as "income support") if they had less than the basic pension. In P&V sector homes, the benefit structure (described later in this chapter) was quite different, yielding much higher amounts than applied in LA homes. For example, in a P&V sector residential care home, the income support level for a member of the residual group still covered by these rules (see below) is, at 1995/6 rates, at least 210-35 per week, compared with the LA care home rate of 58-85. Claimants, moreover, needed only to satisfy the benefit rules: the social security system did not concern itself with the question of whether or not residential care was actually necessary in any particular case.

A significant event took place at the beginning of the period in question when, in 1980, the supplementary benefit system was radically overhauled, wide areas of discretion being replaced with laborious codification into formal regulations. This was intended as a cost-control measure, but the effect of defining entitlements more rigidly, in order to limit them, is also to make them more explicit and thus sometimes easier to claim. Payments in respect of care homes were firmed up in this way.

It would be a gross over-simplification to attribute the subsequent escalation of supplementary benefit spending in this area merely to this technical change in the rules. Rather, a number of factors were involved: demographic changes which were causing a steep increase in the number of elderly people needing residential care; cuts in local government spending which generated a strong incentive to find other ways of meeting need; the run-down of long-stay hospital care. (See e.g. Land, 1988; Bradshaw, 1988). Whatever the pressures at work, though, there is no doubt that the above changes to social security rules in this area were of great importance in facilitating the expansion of P&V sector care home provision.

The increase in spending was certainly impressive. The community care White Paper, Caring for People, lamented that supplementary benefit/income support costs on P&V sector residential care and nursing homes "...rose in cash terms from 10m. in December 1979 to over 1,000m. by May 1989". (DoH, 1989, para. 8.5). Claimants who were resident at the point of change to the new community care arrangements in April 1993 remain within the old benefit structure. Just over a year later, a DSS Minister again emphasised the scale of the increase in benefit costs: "Income support at the higher levels is paid to 284,000 people in residential care and nursing homes at a cost of 2.7 billion; compared with support for just 12,000 at a cost of 10 million in 1979" (Nicholas Scott, House of Commons Hansard, Written Answers, col. 351, 16 May 1994). Doubtless to enhance the dramatic effect, the Government has not filtered out the effects of ordinary inflation in making these comparisons, but the figures are nevertheless striking.

Benefit Limits and the "Shortfall"

It seems that, when the initial stimulus to the P&V sector began to gather pace in the early 1980s, the Government, being ideologically well-disposed to an increase in private provision, was not greatly dismayed and indeed in that sense welcomed this development. This soon changed, given the steepness of the spending curve, and in 1983 controls on the level of charge which would be met became more stringent, with a new system of local limits. This was followed in 1985 with a severe tightening-up via a system of national limits. These varied by "client group" and type of home, with (after July 1986) slightly higher limits in London. This held back the rate of increase of spending to a degree, but brought with it a further set of problems, in that rigid national limits naturally generated an increase in the number of instances in which benefit payments were not enough to meet the charge levied by the home (an effect which varied considerably around the country, but which was widespread). This "shortfall" question was to become a source of growing controversy and political embarrassment to the Government.

The consequences of the shortfall were often serious for those affected. It was certainly commonplace for personal expenses allowances to be absorbed by the charge, leaving the resident with no spending money (a problem which has not been solved by the new system - see chapter 5). Relatives often felt pressured into finding the money to make up the difference between benefit and charge, sometimes themselves experiencing severe financial difficulty as a consequence. Some homes absorbed the shortfall in whole or in part, which could jeopardise financial viability. Some offered a lower standard of accommodation (e.g. shared rooms) to residents dependent on income support. Many charities faced a steep increase in requests for payments to "top up" deficient benefit levels.

These various ill-effects (which were by no means mutually exclusive) were well-documented, grave concern being expressed both inside and outside Parliament (Age Concern, 1989; House of Commons Social Services Committee, 1990a; House of Commons Social Security Committee, 1991; National Association of Citizens' Advice Bureaux, 1991). Since April 1993, these problems are not supposed to arise in respect of new residents (again, though, see chapter 5 for a note of caution). However, people who were P&V sector care home residents at the end of March 1993 have been kept within the old benefit regime and for them the position is largely unchanged.

The issue of the "shortfall", as it became increasingly problematic and politically embarrassing, served to intensify the DSS belief that here was an area of provision which ought to be transferred to somebody else. The DSS's escapological ambitions, moreover, chimed in with developments elsewhere which also pointed towards change.

Pressure for Change

The growing role of P&V sector residential and nursing care was accompanied by a professional debate as to what was the appropriate response to the increasing number of people with care requirements; and intensifying criticism of the deployment of large amounts of social security money in this area without any assessment of individual need. A series of official reports appeared: the Audit Commission (1986) condemned the financial lack of focus; the Firth Report (1987) set out the deliberations of a joint central/local government working party which had been examining similar issues; the Wagner Report (1988) examined overall policy towards residential care; and the Griffiths Report (1988) made bold proposals for reorganisation of the allocation of resources for care services. An interweaving of themes developed: "good practice" in relation to community care; the prudent use of public money; and the DSS's desire to extricate itself from this area of provision.

The Griffiths enquiry, in particular, had carried with it the Government's hopes for a solution to the problem which would be both workable and ideologically acceptable. In this latter respect, there were worries about the central role which Griffiths envisaged for local authority SSDs. The Government was not above transferring problematic areas of service delivery to LAs, as evidenced by the history of the housing benefit scheme (see Fimister and Hill, 1993). But housing benefit was very tightly controlled from the centre, in a way which would not be practicable in the case of community care. As central government policy generally aimed to weaken, rather than enhance, the powers of local authorities, some time was spent after the Griffiths Report was published in trying to find an alternative agency to play the key organising role: but nothing practicable emerged, so eventually the White Paper appeared, taking on board the main thrust of Griffiths's proposals.

The New System Replaces the Old

The new arrangements for the finance and organisation of community care were originally intended for April 1991, but in the event were deferred until April 1993. Officially, the delay was to give LAs and Health Authorities enough time to be adequately prepared, although some believe that the possible effect on poll tax levels in the run-up to a General Election was also a factor. It seems likely that there is an element of truth in both contentions.

Under the new regime, as noted in chapter 1, lead responsibility for the finance, design and co-ordination of community care packages was given to local authority SSDs. There is a strong emphasis on collaboration with other agencies, notably health services and P&V sector care providers, but also including others such as housing providers (recognition of the importance of the latter having been somewhat belated). Additional resources, representing the social security savings from the new system, have been transferred to SSDs (see chapter 3 for a discussion of the scope and adequacy of this provision). Encouragement of the private sector is a persistent theme, various financial mechanisms having been put in place to exert pressure on SSDs to this end (see chapter 5).

While the new system is intended to lay greater emphasis than the old on more imaginative care packages, with less ready recourse to residential options, the finance of residential and nursing home care nevertheless remains of crucial importance. I shall explore later in this chapter the parallel history of social security in relation to supported lodgings, hostels and similar forms of provision; while the issues around benefits and non-residential care are examined especially in chapters 5 and 6. Let us continue for the moment, though, to focus on residential care and nursing homes.

1.   Residential care and nursing homes: pre-April 1993.

The new system is very different to that which it has replaced. Before April 1993, residential care and nursing homes were treated in two different ways for social security purposes, depending on whether they were LA homes or provided in the P&V sector. (As regards the latter, I am concerned here with P&V sector homes which were registered with the social services or health registration authority; and some smaller, unregistered homes whose level of care provision led them to be treated for benefit purposes as if they were registered).

As explained earlier in this chapter, the formula for LA homes was based on the standard retirement pension and the benefit outlay was relatively modest, income support only coming into play if other income was below pension level. SSDs would charge residents at least the "minimum charge", equivalent to four-fifths of the pension. (I describe here the standard arrangements: they could exceptionally be varied). Income above the retirement pension figure was also deemed to be available towards the cost, leaving the resident with a personal expenses allowance of one fifth of basic pension level (plus, in the case of better-off residents, any surplus income over and above the cost of the accommodation). There was a formula to take account of the value of savings and other capital assets. This charging framework also applied if the SSD chose to "sponsor" (that is, take financial responsibility for) a resident in a P&V sector home -

although the number of instances where this happened declined greatly as the role of supplementary benefit in the P&V sector grew.

If, on the other hand, the home was in the P&V sector, income support - topping up any other income and again with capital taken into account - would meet the charge up to a fixed limit, the latter varying with category of need and type of home. For example, a "very dependent elderly" person in a residential care home would be entitled to have charges met up to 227-00 per-week. (Although we are talking about the old system, this is the "out-of-London" rate for 1995/6: it should be remembered that this system continues for those who were resident at the point of change, or who would have been but for a temporary absence). The corresponding figure for a "mentally disordered" person in a nursing home would be 296-00. These are examples drawn from more than a dozen categories in the two types of home. A small personal expenses allowance, slightly higher than that normally permitted to LA care home residents, was also payable. The fixed limits, of course, gave rise to the "shortfall" problem discussed above.

The treatment of attendance allowance (AA) and the care component of disability living allowance (DLAC) (see chapter 3 for a brief description of these) also varied between sectors, although the effects on claimants' incomes were much the same. AA and DLAC normally stopped after 28 days for LA home residents. They continued to be payable for those in P&V sector homes, but were offset against income support entitlement. The mobility component of disability living allowance (DLAM) (again, see chapter 3) was - and remains - disregarded in both sectors.

2. The "preserved group".

For those P&V sector residents who remain within the old system, the danger of the income support shortfall continues -which is why the term "preserved rights", applied to this group, is so misleading, as it sounds so positive! It is true that "preservation" in the old system could be an advantage to some who might wish to remain in residential care but who might not be assessed as needing it by the SSD under the new arrangements. Generally, though, "preserved rights" are likely to be either neutral or disadvantageous. It should be noted that these rules apply to those normally resident at the time of changeover in April 1993, even though some will not yet be claiming income support, perhaps because their capital resources are still too high. It is difficult to escape from the preserved group: one has to be out of residential or nursing home care for more than 13 weeks (permanent residents), four weeks (temporary residents) or 52 weeks (if in hospital) in order to break the link and have access to the new system (see below).

Otherwise, if the resident is caught by the shortfall, SSDs can only help in limited circumstances. As was the case under the old system, they can "top up" deficient income support payments only for those under pension age (or where an established topping-up arrangement existed before the resident reached that age). If these circumstances do not apply, the SSD can help a person in a residential care home to try to find another suitable home with fees within the income support limits but, if this is not possible, can only take financial responsibility and admit him or her into the new system in cases of genuine eviction or home closure. (To prevent "bluff" on the part of the proprietor, a move is necessary: the resident cannot be supported by the SSD under the new rules in the same home or in one operated by the same owner). In cases where residents are helped by the SSD because of eviction or closure, "preserved group" levels of benefit remain payable, but the SSD has a duty to meet the cost of the home, applying "new scheme" assessment and charging rules (see below).

In the case of "preserved group" residents over pension age caught up in nursing home evictions and closures, SSDs - although again able to help to look for a cheaper home - do not have the power to take financial responsibility. Here, the duty of last resort lies with the NHS. (During consultations on guidance, the LA Associations had strenuously to insist upon a mention of the NHS role in this area). The problem in relation to nursing homes arises not only where the resident was in such a home at the point of change to the new system, but also where he or she was in a P&V sector residential care home but has subsequently moved to a nursing home. Thus, a previously affordable situation can fall foul of the DSS limits because the resident's dependency has increased, with the added complication of the lack of powers to step in on the part of the SSD. This is a growing cause for concern at the time of writing.

These various restrictions on SSDs' powers in relation to the "preserved group" are intended to prevent the siphoning-off of a large proportion of the funds available for community care in order to top up inadequate income support payments. It is believed that the DoH pressed for the continuation of the "no topping up above pension age" rule, against the wishes of the DSS. Nevertheless, the effect has been to continue the uncertainty and insecurity of the "shortfall" for a large number of vulnerable residents. Although this group is obviously declining in number as residents die, the Government's inability to deal with the problem remains a very disappointing aspect of the recent changes.

3. Residential care and nursing homes: from April 1993.

Residents who enter P&V sector residential care or nursing homes from April 1993 onwards fall under a very different regime. They receive something like ordinary social security benefits, except that AA and DLAC now normally stop after 28 days (unless the resident is not being financially supported by the SSD, in which case they continue to be paid); and there is a special income support addition called the "residential allowance"(57-00 in Greater London, 51-00 elsewhere, at 1995/6 rates).The residential allowance represented a late change of plan: it had originally been intended to allow HB to be paid to P&V sector residents in respect of their accommodation costs, but considerable disagreement between and amongst the different central government departments and LA associations as to the appropriate formula led, after a lengthy stalemate, to the emergence of an income support-based solution instead.

It should be remembered that not all care home residents will look to support from the SSD in order to enter residential or nursing home care: those who are sufficiently affluent will be able to purchase a place privately. Fundamental to the new system, though, is the idea that SSDs, through their assessments of care needs, should act as "gatekeepers" of public funds in this area. If a care home is considered the right care solution, then the SSD will pay the cost of the placement and levy a charge upon the resident's resources. The charging structure is based broadly on the income support rules, the resident being required to pay anything up to the full cost of the placement, depending on the level of his or her income and capital. As under the old system, a modest personal expenses allowance is permitted. The question of charging for care is considered further in later chapters, especially chapter 5.

At the time of writing, a certain amount of controversy is taking place around a "loophole" in the rules as regards the SSD's gatekeeping role. The DSS's intention had been that AA and DLAC would not be payable to P&V sector residents unless they were "self-financing", meaning that they were not receiving income support, HB or financial support from the

SSD. However, the DSS has fallen foul of the complexity of its own regulations and now admits that the policy intention has not been achieved: if the resident can steer clear of LA involvement, then AA or DLAC can still be paid even if he or she receives income support. This permits the income support severe disability premium to be paid (see chapter 3) which, together with the residential allowance, may enable the resident to assemble a package of benefits which is enough to pay for a care home place at the lower end of the price range (a possibility which varies around the country). This bypasses the SSD's rationing role and can be financially advantageous to some claimants, mainly in circumstances where they have a house to sell (because of certain differences between the income support and SSD means tests in their treatment of capital). A legal debate is under way as to the extent to which SSDs may or may not have a liability to identify and advise upon such cases. I do not intend to pursue this question further in these pages, given its highly technical nature and the strong possibility that the DSS will have plugged the loophole by the time this book appears: but readers may wish to take advice from a welfare rights specialist if they encounter this problem and are unsure of the position.

The new system in relation to LA homes has changed much less. (I am concerned here with conventional LA residential care homes provided under Part 111 of the National Assistance Act 1948, as amended by the NHS and Community Care Act 1990. I am not, for the moment, referring to those LA projects for "less dependent" people which, since April 1993, have fallen under the same legislation. They are treated differently for benefit purposes, as long as board is not provided: see "hostels" below; and the typology of accommodation in chapter 4). For the purposes of charging in LA residential care homes, the four fifths/ one fifth arrangement in relation to the basic retirement pension figure remains almost intact, the proportions having changed slightly as the personal expenses allowance (previously, as noted above, a little lower for LA residents) has been aligned with that in the P&V sector. The main change lies in the rules for the definition of available income and capital, which - as in the case of P&V sector homes - have for the most part been aligned with the income support scheme. The income support level for residents of LA homes, however, continues to be aligned with the basic retirement pension (58-85 per week at 1995/6 rates): there are no premiums and there is no residential allowance. AA and DLAC stop after 28 days, even for people who are paying the full cost of their place.

The reason for continuing with a much lower level of benefit support for LA residents is to create what the government calls an incentive to SSDs to use the P&V sector; or, as LAs would put it, a penalty for using their own homes. This is because the lower benefits mean that they recoup much less through the charging system in the latter case. This is explored in more detail in chapter 5.

Respite Care and other Temporary Placements

When a person enters a residential care or nursing home, it does not necessarily mean that this is intended as a permanent move. Periods of planned respite care, usually to give a carer a break, are by definition temporary; while there are many other reasons why a stay might be intended from the outset to be for a limited period - perhaps because the resident's health is improving after an operation or a transient setback, or while accommodation in the community is adapted or a move finalised.

I shall not attempt here to explore the detailed history of the benefit rules as they apply to temporary placements in LA or P&V sector care homes. Suffice it to say that they have never been straightforward and the post-April 1993 arrangements have introduced new difficulties. Especially in the P&V sector, this is an area which has proved particularly confusing for claimants, carers and community care practitioners, as will be apparent from the quirks and complexities described in chapter 3.

The "Middle Ground"

A very important area of community care provision is the middle ground between residential care on the one hand and largely independent living in one's own home on the other. I refer to supported lodgings; "adult placement" or "adult fostering" schemes; group homes and hostels. Such options have become increasingly important to thinking and practice in the community care field. While the events described above were unfolding in the area of residential and nursing home care, a parallel process of change was going on as regards benefit provision for these generally smaller-scale, "mid-way" projects. I would like now to backtrack this narrative to look at this aspect of the story.

1.   Supported lodgings.

Again, supplementary benefit played a significant role, with special formulae which applied to people in board and lodging and hostel accommodation (whether or not they had community care needs). Ominously, though, these provisions were more expensive and more difficult to administer than ordinary benefit entitlements. The general field of board and lodging payments had, moreover, proved (like care home costs) to be dogged by political difficulty from the Government's point of view: attempts to contain costs through a system of limits; inadequate annual upratings; punitive limits on the duration of benefit for young people; several legal challenges to the regulations...again, all of these combined to convince social security Ministers that here was a system best transferred elsewhere.

In November 1986, DHSS officials informed the LA Associations that the board and lodging formula was to be abolished in April 1988, at the same time as supplementary benefit was to be replaced with income support. (In the event, the board and lodging changes were deferred until April 1989).Instead, claimants would receive ordinary income support and would claim HB towards their housing costs. In abstract principle, there was something to be said for "normalising" the benefit status of a marginal group of claimants; but in practice, there were problems which appeared not to have been considered by the DHSS. In particular, there was the question of how claimants would pay for elements in the accommodation charge which were ineligible for HB, such as meals, fuel, water and care costs. If claimants were expected to meet these out of their income support, then where benefit levels were particularly low (notably in the case of young people) or where ineligible charges were particularly high (notably in the case of care costs), a boarder could be left with very little disposable income after paying the charge - or even none at all in those cases where the charge was greater than the claimant's entire income. The implications for supported lodgings and similar projects (where, of course, care costs can be substantial) were serious. While there would be "gainers" as well as "losers", many of the latter could be left in an untenable situation.

Interestingly, in 1986, the Social Security side of the then Department of Health and Social Security did not seem to be aware of the existence and role of supported lodgings; while the Health side (which had policy responsibility for personal social services matters) did not seem to be aware of the benefit proposals until after they had been formulated. (A senior official on the Health wing once took me to task for alleging such a lack of communication, which she disputed, but another confirmed my impression). Certainly, there was no mention of supported lodgings in the December consultative document (DHSS, 1986). As criticism mounted, the Government commissioned research on supported lodgings from the Office of Population Censuses and Surveys (Young, 1988). This confirmed the problem, but the DHSS pressed on with the proposals regardless. Unofficially, the attitude seemed to be that, since a number of LAs already funded such schemes themselves to one degree or another, then LAs could be expected to bail out any casualties. This was a sensitive subject at a time when the Government was still agonising over its response to Griffiths, but eventually the point was made explicit by a Minister in the Lords:

"Research shows that just over half of those local authorities which run schemes already fund them in whole or in part. They will continue to be able to fund them after next April. The consideration is entirely as it always has been - in the lap of local authorities". (Lord Skelmersdale, House of Lords Hansard, col. 146, Nov. 1988).

Other issues followed on from the supported lodgings controversy. During 1987, the degree of care which defined for benefit purposes a small, unregistered residential home was altered, reducing to supported lodging levels the benefits payable in a number of cases where the amount and type of care provided had previously been enough to attract "care home" rates of supplementary benefit. Some schemes sponsored by health authorities were also finding their clients designated as hospital patients, greatly reducing benefits payable (a "boundary problem" of which more is said in chapter 4). It seemed clear that the DHSS was intensifying its efforts to push care costs out of the benefit system, an impression borne out by developments in relation to hostels.

2. Hostels.

Hostels (see appendix 3 for the sense in which the term is used in this book) again represent an important area of provision as part of an overall community care strategy. They vary a good deal in their "client groups" and funding, but many provide a significant level of personal care, the costs of which were included, up until October 1989, in a special supplementary benefit/income support formula.

The December 1986 consultative document on board and lodging payments had also said that the rules relating to benefits for hostel-dwellers would be reviewed at some stage. The definition of "hostel" subsequently adopted by the DHSS for this purpose was: "broadly...any accommodation which is not self-contained and is managed by a registered housing association; or is non-commercial and funded by a government body or a local authority; or is managed by a voluntary body or charity for the purpose of rehabilitation or resettlement within the community". This definition was taken from the income support regulations, which also provided "a discretionary power to treat similar properties as hostels". (DSS, 1988, para. 1.2).

Once more, research was commissioned, this time from the Policy Studies Institute (Berthoud and Casey, 1988a) and again its findings - that often substantial care costs were involved - were ignored. Indeed, in this case it is fair to say that the findings were rather badly misrepresented, to the extent that the researchers found it necessary to rebut Ministers' version(Berthoud and Casey, 1988b). The Government pressed ahead with an "ordinary income support plus HB" model, to be introduced from October 1989. This applied to LA, as well as non-LA hostels, except that in the former case, those which provided board were to be re-designated for benefit purposes as LA residential care homes, with the attendant minimal entitlement. (Later, at the time of the April 1993 changes, those which did not provide board- and so from October 1989 had attracted HB - almost suffered the same fate. In the event, though, the LA Associations were able to negotiate the preservation of their "HB status").

Again, considerable disquiet ensued, this time from within the Conservative Party as well as from more obvious sources. The Government was not willing to back down on the essentials of the proposals, but made some concessions on the transitional arrangements, in both LA and non-LA sectors. Whereas in the case of board and lodging, a degree of transitional protection (preservation of current entitlements) was offered to existing claimants, this was extended this time to the revenues of the hostels and LAs themselves, to bridge the gap between October 1989 and April 1991, when the finances concerned would be handed over to "traditional funding agencies". For the most part, this meant that SSDs would from that time be expected to take responsibility, the DSS funds being distributed amongst them in financial year 1991/2 by means of the "Revenue Support Grant", the standard vehicle for central government grant aid to LAs and one which has no mechanism for the identification of the geographical location of hostels. In other words, the distribution of the money bore no relationship to the whereabouts of the hostels: but no matter, the DSS was now free of the irksome hostels formula, which was the main thing.

Hostels and supported lodgings projects of one kind and another responded to these various upheavals by seeking whatever alternative funding could be found and by making renewed efforts to maximise claimants' uptake of benefit entitlements. In particular, AA and (from April 1992) DLAC, the severe disability premium within income support and the possibility, in some circumstances, of claiming HB to meet charges for general support and counselling (but not personal care) have been pursued. (See chapter 3 for a more detailed discussion of these various benefits). The end result has been a complex pattern of gainers and losers (see Noble and Smith, 1993, for some conclusions based on research in Birmingham and Oxford).

The next set of problems to beset "middle ground" provision arose in the run-up to the April 1993 changes and concerned the question of registration of what are often misleadingly referred to as "small homes".

Registration Becomes a Hazard

This time, the issue has been the frontier in the P&V sector between small residential care homes and projects where a higher degree of independence on the part of the resident is envisaged. Prior to April 1993, those projects which attracted the higher "care home" rates of income support were differentiated from those which attracted "ordinary" benefits, including HB, by means of a detailed test of the level and type of care provided. This "care test" was complex and difficult to administer. However, since April 1993, as a result of amendment of the care homes legislation, "small homes" - those with fewer than four residents - have had to be registered with social services or health registration authorities if they provide both board and personal care (unless all residents have lived there for longer than five years). "Fewer than four" is intended literally, meaning as few as one. Here, the DSS saw a vehicle for considerable simplification within benefit administration: it was announced that, from April 1993, registration would mark the "dependency" boundary, instead of the care test.

The "higher income support" regime prior to April 1993 was frequently favoured by "small home" proprietors, who saw it as financially advantageous. This advantage was not always as great as was supposed, since levels of HB applicable to accommodation which fell short of the care test criteria, but which offered substantial support services, could also be high. For residents, there was the additional question of how much disposable income remained after paying the home's fees, where the HB regime might compare favourably with the income support personal expenses allowance, depending on the level of ineligible charges. The different rules and practices on benefit limits applied by the income support scheme and HB authorities added a further layer of complication.

Under the new arrangements, though, the higher "care home" rates of income support were being phased out, leaving only the relatively modest residential allowance in their place. Future residents of registered "small homes" would need to look to the SSD to make up the difference. This was consistent with the treatment of larger registered homes and financially unproblematic for proprietors if the SSD agreed that the care need required its intervention and that the placement was appropriate and acceptably priced. It could indeed be advantageous where the income support care home limits would otherwise have been a problem. The change could be similarly neutral or - because of the previous limits - advantageous for residents whose accommodation would have "passed" the care test under the old rules.

However, in the cases of "less dependent" residents who would have been able to claim HB under the old rules but who were now caught on the wrong side of the "registration" divide, the change brought a major financial hazard to the individuals concerned, as well as additional costs to SSDs which the latter had not anticipated. There would be considerable loss of benefit, as new claimants would be unable to obtain HB and - as a result of SSD financial involvement - would lose entitlement to AA or DLAC and consequently to the income support severe disability premium. The only disposable income allowed might well be the residential care personal expenses allowance. (See chapter 4 for a full discussion of these effects).

The problem was that the very broad scope of the registration criteria would draw in a large number of supported lodging-type situations and certain types of hostel which were not intended as care homes in which residents would be highly dependent. The LA Associations believed that the DSS had simply failed to appreciate the potential scope of registration and that, once the matter had been explained, the proposals would be withdrawn. Detailed briefings, including worked-out examples, were provided; but, although it is no doubt true that the Department had not initially appreciated the consequences, an explanation of them was not enough to persuade the DSS to forgo the administrative advantage upon which it had set its sights. The LA Associations therefore proposed a simplified version of the care test, but the DSS stuck to its guns. The DoH was also fully briefed by the Associations but (possibly to its subsequent regret) was unwilling to engage with what it saw as a social security matter. The chaotic consequences of the "registration test" are fully explored in chapter 4.

In reflecting upon the changes to benefit regimes which have overtaken these "middle ground" forms of provision, it is difficult to escape the conclusion that, where the DSS agenda collides with the interests of community care service users, the latter are likely to come off a poor second.

Recent Experience

The first two years of the new system have thrown up a number of problems, of varying degrees of magnitude and complexity, in relation both to benefit and to charging matters and across the range of types of accommodation, as well as domiciliary and day care provision.

I have several times had occasion to chronicle the history of the welfare rights aspects of the community care changes (Fimister, 1988, 1991 and 1993a; Fimister and Hill, 1993). In updating the tale for this book, I am happily able to record that one element which has changed for the better is an improved recognition on the part of the DSS and DoH of the need to identify and try to address at least the more minor difficulties brought to light by the process of change. This has its limitations: solutions with a significant financial cost are generally ruled out; nor has there been any rush to correct past misdeeds, such as the "registration test". But there is to a degree a more ready appreciation of the tangle which can easily result in the benefit and charging field if a wide view of the many strands is not taken. This was not always the case. In October 1989, the month before the publication of the community care White Paper, the first of a series of meetings took place which were to develop into a central/local government forum for the monitoring and discussion of the planning and development of the new community care arrangements. (This has since developed into the Joint Social Services Group, with a wider remit which also takes in children's issues). At the first meeting, the AMA tabled a list of social security matters which needed to be addressed. The suggestion was met with some dismay, the DoH insisting that bilateral discussions should be held instead between the DSS and the LA Associations. In the event, the DSS rejected all of the Associations' proposals by post, saving the trouble of calling a meeting.

From then on, however, the LA Associations and the central government departments have received a steady stream of enquiries from service users, carers, voluntary organisations, local authorities, health professionals, Members of Parliament, the media and others, experience serving to demonstrate that the path would be far from smooth and that problems relating to benefits and charging could not safely be ignored. In due course, a "Benefits and Charging Group" was set up, as a technical sub-group of the Joint Social Services Group. Chaired by the DSS, its ethos is as helpful and constructive as tight budgetary constraints will allow.

Nevertheless, the usefulness of such discussions often lies in clarifying problems more than in finding solutions to them. The latter are likely to be achieved only where there is little or no cost - as is sometimes the case in technical, organisational and administrative matters. Improvements in such areas can be very helpful, but unfortunately for service users and their carers, progress on most issues of substance costs money.

This returns us to a theme touched upon in chapter 1: that is, that "the community" can be an unfriendly place for those who are vulnerable in some respect. It can be difficult at the best of times to get by on the very low incomes provided by social security benefits; debts - including those arising from the Social Fund - can push people below even this level; decent housing and, for those in the labour market, stable employment with even minimally adequate wages can be hard to secure. Moreover, the Government's current review of social security has, at the time of writing, yielded legislation to replace invalidity benefit with "incapacity benefit" (from April 1995) which, it is intended, will be much harder to get; legislation to replace unemployment benefit (from October 1996) with a much more limited "job seeker's allowance"; and proposals for substantial cuts in HB (from October 1995) for many deregulated private sector and housing association tenants. By the time this book appears, it is quite possible that yet more cuts will have been announced in one or other part of the benefit system. Community care clients cannot hope to be unaffected by all of this.

Chapter 3

The Benefits and the Financial Structure

Summary

The new community care system entails a major commitment of public resources and interacts extensively with the social security system. This chapter explores the financial mechanisms which underpin the new approach, with particular reference to the role of social security benefits. The chapter commences by describing the most relevant benefits; and concludes with an examination of how these feed into community care finance.

The Benefits

In order to follow the detail of this and later chapters, it is necessary to have at least an outline knowledge of the main benefits which community care service users may receive. Obviously, these are not in general peculiar to the community care context, but most service users will be entitled to at least one (and frequently more than one) of them. Some readers will already have a broad understanding of the benefits concerned and some will indeed be social security specialists. However, others will have a more limited knowledge and there will be, moreover, some overseas readers who are not familiar with the United Kingdom context. I shall therefore provide an outline sketch. In the process, I shall attempt to draw out some of the issues which relate specifically to community care - which should provide enough complexity to hold the attention even of the benefits expert.

I should emphasise that *the following is not intended in any sense as a welfare rights guide*. A number of good, detailed guides are available. Information on most of them can be obtained from the Child Poverty Action Group, which markets a range of rights handbooks including several of those produced by other organisations. Enquiries should be made to CPAG, currently at: 4th. Floor, 1-5 Bath Street, London, EC1V 9PY.

Telephone 0171-2533406. My own preference is to use CPAG's National Welfare Benefits Handbook (CPAG, 1995a) as a "way in" to the legislation(this is a guide to means-tested benefits which provides detailed references to legislation, official guidance and case law)supplemented by the Disability Alliance's Disability Rights Handbook (Disability Alliance, 1995) (which has more extensive coverage of disability-related benefits). For non-means-tested benefits, I would recommend CPAG's Rights Guide to Non-Means-Tested Benefits (CPAG, 1995b). Volumes of annotated legislation can also be purchased from CPAG; while users of computerised benefit-checking systems (see chapter 6) will find the growing sophistication of the "help screens" useful for back-up information.

I shall begin this brief review of the main benefits with:

National Insurance and Related Benefits

"National insurance" benefits are based on contributions paid (or, in certain circumstances, "credited" without having been paid). Contrary to popular belief, they are not based on "insurance" principles: there is no individual assessment of risk- the contributions are, in effect, an earmarked (or "hypothecated") tax. They are in most respects not means-tested and the required contribution record varies from one benefit to another, often entailing quite complicated formulae. There are also some non-contributory and non-means-tested benefits which perform similar functions for those (generally disabled people or carers) who have not had an opportunity to build up adequate contribution records. These are paid at lower levels and usually have very restrictive access criteria.

Retirement pension is the most widespread national insurance benefit. It is normally paid from age 60 for women and 65 for men (although the Government intends to equalise pension ages at 65 by the year 2020). Its basic level (given at 1995/6 rates, as are all benefit figures in this book) is 58-85 per week. "Younger" pensioners are increasingly likely to have pension income above the basic rate: some will have earnings-related pensions from the state earnings-related pension scheme established in the 1970s (and/or its more limited predecessor). Many others will have occupational or personal pensions generated outside the state scheme (albeit with substantial public subsidy). On the other hand, a small number of older pensioners with deficient contribution records receive a modest non-contributory pension (up to 35-25 per week).

Incapacity benefit (basic long-term rate 58-85 per week; there are lower, short-term rates and also certain possible additions) is payable to people who are not capable of work because of illness or disability. There is a lower, non-contributory version called *severe disablement allowance* (basic rate 35-55, again with possible additions). The demand for an earnings replacement benefit for people who are long-term sick or disabled naturally reflects, to a degree, the state of the labour market. People do not fit readily into two clear-cut categories, either fully fit or completely incapable of work: there is a continuum. In the middle ground, there are those whose job opportunities will be highly sensitive to the overall demand for labour in the economy. This is obviously important in the community care context. There are many people with physical or learning disabilities or mental illness (including those who are recovering from a mental illness) whose employment prospects will be especially liable to fluctuate with the economic situation, given that they will tend to be in a relatively weaker position to compete in times of job shortage. Sustained high unemployment since the early 1980s caused the numbers on invalidity benefit, the precursor of incapacity benefit, to rise substantially, as people remained on benefit for longer periods. The Government responded to this by introducing incapacity benefit, from April 1995, to replace invalidity benefit (and its short-term variant, sickness benefit). The new benefit has stricter and more explicitly "medical" eligibility criteria than did invalidity benefit (also extended to severe disablement allowance and some income support claimants) which are intended to bring about a major reduction in the number of beneficiaries. Displacement of incapacity-related benefits by unemployment-related benefits is a serious business for those concerned, given that the latter of these, in order not to compete with very low wages, are kept at minimal levels.

Invalid care allowance is a benefit designed for those whose caring responsibilities keep them out of full-time employment. It is non-contributory and paid at a low rate (35-25 per week). Narrow criteria mean that many carers are not eligible. This is a benefit which has great relevance and potential as part of a community care strategy, but it has been neglected as the state has continued to try to keep carers' labour on a largely unremunerated basis. This issue is explored further in chapter 7.

Unemployment benefit (normally 46-45) is potentially relevant to those community care service users who are able to work. Strict contribution conditions and a time limit (one year)on the duration of claims mean that the majority of unemployed people do not receive this benefit. Entitlement will diminish further from October 1996, when the Government proposes to replace it with the *jobseeker's allowance*, the non-means-tested element of which will last only for six months (essentially an elaborate way of halving the duration of unemployment benefit under cover of a name change). The low proportion of claimants receiving the non-means-tested element may well at some future stage be used as an excuse to propose its abolition. Other conditions for the receipt of unemployment-related benefits(including means-tested income support for unemployed people)have steadily been tightened in recent years, with increasingly severe penalties for labour indiscipline (alleged failure "actively" to seek work; alleged leaving of a job "without just cause"; and so on). This process is set to continue with the jobseeker's allowance. Obviously, workers who are more vulnerable (for example because of a disability or present or past mental illness) are going to be more likely to fall foul of aggressive administration.

In the cases of both of the "new" benefits - incapacity benefit and jobseeker's allowance - the Government has taken the legislative opportunity to insert a number of subsidiary cuts: for example, the loss of an earnings-related element in the former case; and the introduction of a lower rate of benefit for younger claimants (as per the income support scheme - see below)in the latter.

All of the above benefits have rules which allow for *additional payments in respect of "dependants"*, although the criteria vary and are sometimes very restrictive.

The above are also benefits which are intended to substitute for earnings, so in most cases the latter will affect the amount payable. *Some earnings are allowed*, although the amount varies greatly from one benefit to another; and there is sometimes a stipulation that the work must be "therapeutic".

If a claimant goes into hospital, the above benefits will be reduced by various different amounts at different stages, again varying between benefits: the details are complex and a rights guide should be consulted as necessary. *If a claimant goes into a care home*, these benefits are not affected as a direct consequence (although in the cases of unemployment benefit and especially invalid care allowance, it is of course likely that the claimant - that is, an unemployed person or carer who has him or herself gone into a care home - will not be able to meet the wider conditions of eligibility). If the care home place is funded by the SSD, then charges will be levied against the resident's benefits.

I shall go on now to consider the system of means-tested social assistance which sometimes supplements and sometimes replaces national insurance and similar benefits.

Income Support

Income support is a means-tested benefit which, broadly, represents the amount which the state is prepared to make available to people who are not in full-time work (defined as 16 hours or more per week) to top up their incomes to a basic level.(There are in fact various groups which are not covered, such as certain people from abroad and most students; and there are numerous deductions which can reduce claimants below the supposed minimum, but the above describes the general idea)."Requirements" are worked out, consisting of a basic living allowance plus various additions, most of which are called "premiums" (see below). "Resources" are then calculated according to a very detailed set of rules and are compared with "requirements". If "resources" are lower than "requirements", then the difference is payable as income support. There is a complex formula for including capital (but not the home in which a claimant lives) in the resources figure. Some housing costs not met by housing benefit - notably mortgage interest payments - are allowed (albeit often only in part) as requirements.

The basic living allowance for any adult aged 25 or over is, at current rates, 46-50 per week, with lower amounts for younger people. Rates are different for people treated as couples and there are additions for dependent children. (Again, see a rights guide for full details).

The premiums included in the requirements figure are set out below. Most of them "overlap" - that is, if a person qualifies for more than one, the highest is paid. However, some can be added together: the family, disabled child's, carer's and severe disability premiums are not set off against each other or against other premiums.

Premium	Amount per week
Family.	10-25
Disabled child.	19-80
Lone parent.	5-20
Carer.	12-60
Disability.	19-80
Severe disability.	35-05
Pensioner.	18-60
Enhanced pensioner.	20-70
Higher pensioner.	25-15

These are the "single" rates: in some cases there are different rules and rates for people treated as couples.

This structure was introduced in April 1988, when income support replaced the earlier social assistance scheme, supplementary benefit. The premiums take the place both of the previous "long-term rate" (for long-term claimants other than the unemployed) and of additional weekly payments made to certain claimants for extra needs (mostly related to health or disability).

Astonishingly, people who are literally homeless do not receive premiums. The argument is that their lack of domestic expenses removes the need. This may seem harsh but logical, until one reflects that roofless people have other needs which will cause them additional expense - for example diet, or wear and tear on clothing.

The severe disability premium deserves particular note in the community care context. Introduced as a result of controversy during the passage of the legislation which ushered in the 1988 changes (when supplementary benefit was replaced by income support) this premium was intended to provide compensation for the loss of additional payments, notably for domestic assistance, under the old scheme. It was designed to be difficult to get: not only was a very substantial degree of disablement required(entitlement being based on receipt of attendance allowance or similar benefits); and not only was a person debarred if someone was receiving invalid care allowance in respect of him or her; but claimants were also required to pass what we might term the "isolation test" - that is, they must not be living with any non-dependant aged 18 or over. Since the introduction of this premium, there has been a running battle between the DSS and welfare rights agencies over the exact meaning of the isolation criteria, claimants and their advisers seeking to secure a liberal definition and the Department trying to hold the line. The complexity of the arguments do not lend themselves to summary here, but suffice it to say that the Government has changed the law (several times) to achieve its original restrictive intention, although much additional benefit was gained in the interim and numerous appeals relating to superseded rules are still outstanding at the time of writing.

The severe disability premium has also presented problems in terms of failure on the part of the Benefits Agency (BA) to spot entitlement (see Vaux, 1994, pp 146-7) and of miscalculation once entitlement has been identified (see the example later in this chapter).

It should be noted that the commercial relationship between a landlord or landlady and a lodger does not offend against the isolation requirement, which means that people in supported lodgings - including where there is more than one lodger - can receive the severe disability premium if they satisfy the other criteria. This makes it a very important provision in the context of community care. It also means that somebody moving into a P&V sector care home can become newly entitled to the premium for any period during which attendance allowance and the disability living allowance care component remain in payment (see below) -although I am sure that this possibility is frequently missed.

Again, there are limited *"disregards" of earnings* which income support claimants may have.

If a claimant goes into hospital, income support is reduced at different stages according to a detailed formula. *If a claimant goes into a care home*, the effect on income support depends on whether it is a local authority home, or one located in the P&V sector. In the former case, income support requirements are reduced to the standard retirement pension level, as described in chapter 2. Conversely, in the P&V sector, income support requirements are increased because - again as described in the previous chapter - the residential allowance is added on (and sometimes, as noted above, because of a new, if usually temporary, entitlement to the severe disability premium).

Temporary residence in a P&V care home - for example, for respite care - also attracts the residential allowance. This causes administrative problems for all concerned, as fluctuating income support entitlement leaves changes of payments lagging behind events and claimants become embroiled in repeat claims using a long and difficult application form. Where the higher income support requirements mean that a temporary resident is entitled to income support when he or she is in the care home, but not otherwise, then housing benefit also becomes a problem, as entitlement in respect of the claimant's home in the community increases while he or she is getting income support (see below).A new claim for HB is then needed when the temporary stay in the care home ends, using forms which are often even harder to complete than those for income support. A similar problem arises with council tax benefit. At the time of writing, the LA Associations are seeking to agree simplified repeat claims procedures, across all three benefits, with the DSS. The response from the latter has thus far been sympathetic. Meanwhile, it is very unlikely that the system is working in practice as it is supposed to in theory.

We have already seen in chapter 2 that income support requirements for people in P&V sector residential care and nursing homes used, under the old system, to be far higher.(This remains the case for the "preserved group"). What has happened to the DSS funds freed by the change is a key issue for the financing of the new arrangements (see below).

Benefits for the Extra Costs of Disability

Attendance allowance (AA) and *mobility allowance* (MA)developed in the 1970s to provide some extra support to people who were severely disabled and who incurred additional costs as a consequence. MA, as the name suggests, was concerned with the additional costs resulting from difficulty in getting around. AA is more confusing: historically, it was intended to compensate, at least partially, for the various extra costs of disability - which might include additional heating, dietary or clothing needs, or costs associated with limited shopping opportunities, as well as care costs. Unfortunately, the name has led to a perception of the benefit as being for care costs only, which has become a problem in terms of SSD charging policies (see chapter 5).

In 1992, AA and MA were restructured. Attendance allowance was retained for those who, at the point of change, were aged 65 and over or whose qualifying disability first arises at or above age 65. The corresponding benefit for younger claimants was redesignated and restructured as *disability living allowance (care component)* (DLAC) - an expression which perpetuated the confusion as to its role. MA became *disability living allowance (mobility component)* (DLAM). These benefits are paid at varying rates depending on the degree and type of disability and age at which disability first arises, ranging from 12-40 to 46-70 per-week, or up to 79-35 where both components are payable. They are important to claimants as, not only are they relatively high by social security standards, but they do not normally "overlap" either with each other or with other benefits: that is, they can be added to, rather than offset against, other income. AA and the top or middle rate of DLAC also form part of the entitlement conditions for the severe disability premium within income support, HB and council tax benefit.

If a claimant goes into hospital or a care home, AA and DLAC normally cease after 28 days (although it can be sooner in certain circumstances; while conversely, they can be paid indefinitely to "self-financers" in the P&V sector, a concession which - as noted in chapter 2 - has run into problems of definition). DLAM is not time-limited in this way, which can render it a very important benefit even to highly-dependent care home residents, for - with a bit of imagination - it can make a real difference to a person's quality of life, for example by paying for outings.

Considerable difficulties have arisen during the 1980s and 1990s as the DSS has sought to prevent AA or DLAC from being paid where the Department thinks that SSDs should take financial responsibility. The key parts of the AA and DLAC regulations preclude payment of these benefits where the cost of accommodation is borne wholly or partly by LAs "in pursuance of" various pieces of legislation, including the 1948 National Assistance Act; or where such costs, although not actually met by, "may be borne by", the LA. The open-ended and ambiguous nature of much of this has led to wildly erratic adjudication in supported lodgings and similar circumstances. Not only is there wide variation from one part of the country to another, but it is perfectly possible to find two claimants in identical circumstances living in, say, the same group home, one having been awarded AA or DLAC, the other having had his or her claim disallowed.

Housing (and similar) Benefits

Housing benefit can be very important to people on low incomes, including large numbers who fall within the scope of community care policies. It is a means-tested benefit administered by local housing authorities on behalf of central government. Most (but not all) of the cost is met by the latter, through a very complicated subsidy system. In the case of most private sector lettings, rents have to be referred by the HB authority to the Rent Officer Service, a quasi-autonomous body which decides on the subsidy payable. Some housing association rents are also referred for rent officer scrutiny. HB is based on a formula which uses similar allowances and premiums to income support and which takes into account income, capital and rent level. It can meet up to the full rent, depending not only on the means test itself, but also on whether any "non-dependants" (such as grown-up children or elderly relatives) are assumed to make a contribution and on whether the rent is deemed to be excessive. Claimants on income support automatically "pass" the means test for full rent, although the caveats concerning non-dependants and high rents remain. HB can be paid to people in work, earnings being taken into account as resources, subject to limited disregards.

Supported lodgings and similar accommodation are particularly relevant in the community care context. HB cannot meet charges for board or personal care, but can meet those for general counselling and support in certain circumstances. HB is not payable where the premises are registered with the SSD or the Health Authority as providing residential or nursing care.

If a person goes into a hospital or a care home, HB can still be paid on his or her usual home if the stay is expected to be temporary and (usually) not more than one year. (For "trial periods" in a care home, designed to assess its suitability for the person concerned, the limit is 13 weeks). In practice, though, administrative difficulties can cause payments to cease and advisers need to be alert to this. In the cases of a stay in hospital or a LA care home, the interaction of the different formulae for "downrating" of various benefits can play havoc with HB entitlement. Specialist welfare rights advice will often be needed. In a P&V sector home, HB (as noted earlier in this chapter) can actually go up, because of a new entitlement to income support.

At the time of writing, the Government is planning severe restrictions on HB in respect of above-average rents in the deregulated private rented sector. It is intended that cuts should be introduced to new claims from October 1995 (although it is possible that this timetable may slip). Some housing association places will also be affected. It is unclear at the time of writing how far HB in respect of service charges, including general counselling and support, will be drawn into this. Service charges are in any case currently under review, which could lead to benefit cuts.

The role of HB in relation to community care is explored further in chapter 4.

Council tax benefit (CTB), as the name suggests, is intended to help people on low incomes with council tax payments. It is structured, financed and administered in a very similar way to HB.

A rather confusing tangle of grants exists for the *renovation, improvement, repair and adaptation of an elderly or disabled person's home*. Responsibility is spread awkwardly across SSDs and housing authorities, resulting in some vigorous buck-passing. Moreover, the disabled facilities grant - an important part of this picture - has recently been substantially cut back, the maximum grant having been reduced, with effect from early 1994, from 50,000 to 20,000 (24,000 in Wales). This was, of course, a development highly unwelcome in community care circles (see e.g. Ivory, 1994) and which again exposes the contradictions between the agendas of different government departments - this time with the Department of the Environment(DoE) rather than the DSS as the villain of the piece. Help with home insulation also fits into the jigsaw here. Advisers will want detailed information on all of this, and the coverage in the Disability Rights Handbook (Disability Alliance, 1995) is a good starting point. A recent account of the confused and highly variable situation on the ground, with examples of good as well as bad practice, emerges from research conducted by Bristol University School for Advanced Urban Studies. (Heywood, 1994; and for further commentary, see also George, 1994b).

It might at this point be appropriate to provide *an example of how national insurance and similar benefits, income support, AA/DLAC, HB and CTB relate to each other*. In the process, I shall illustrate the importance of take-up work - a theme explored in detail in chapter 6. The illustration is hypothetical but reflects a type of situation which is often encountered by advice workers (and the mistake referred to at the end occurred in a real instance which the author dealt with on Merseyside -although advisers have met with the same problem elsewhere).

Mrs. Jones is aged 76 and lives alone in a rented council house. She is disabled and frail, but is just about able to continue to live at home with help from her sister and next-door neighbour. Until recently, her weekly income consisted of basic retirement pension and a small widow's pension from her late husband's occupational scheme, together totalling 70-00. She supplemented this by using up her savings. After paying rent and council tax, she was unable to afford to use the heating as much as necessary or to purchase an adequate diet or sufficient warm clothing.

Mrs. Jones's sister persuaded her to ask a welfare rights officer to do a benefit check, with the following results:

- Her income support weekly requirements, without the AA which the benefit check showed she was entitled to (see below), would have been 46-50 basic rate plus enhanced (that is, middle rate) pensioner premium of 20-70. So her total income support requirements would have been 67-20. This is 2-80 less than her current income, so she would not have received any income support - although HB and CTB at just a little less than her full rent and council tax would have been payable.

- However, Mrs. Jones was also entitled to lower rate AA of 31-20, which entitled her to the higher (instead of the enhanced) pensioner premium (25-15) and the severe disability premium (35-05).

- Total weekly benefit entitlement was therefore 137-90 (retirement pension and occupational widow's pension topped up with income support) this last benefit also entitling her to full HB and CTB. Her income support was unaffected by her remaining savings, which were well below the 3,000-00 at which they would have started to reduce it.

- Note that the severe disability premium is paid on top of other premiums and AA is paid on top of all other benefits.

- Note also that the benefit check roughly doubled Mrs. Jones's income and eliminated her outgoings on rent and council tax.

All was not plain sailing, though, with Mrs. Jones's claims: the local BA office reduced her severe disability premium by the amount of her higher pensioner premium, instead of adding the two together, and it needed the intervention of the welfare rights adviser to sort this out. In the process, it emerged that the office was doing this with all similar claims, so the adviser asked that a trawl should be done, wherever possible, of all previous wrong decisions (not all of which, regrettably, would have been identifiable).

The benefits described above by no means constitute a complete list of those available. There are separate systems for *industrial and war disablement*; there are *low-wage supplements* (family credit and disability working allowance) - particularly relevant to those community care service users who are working, since their earnings will often be limited by illness or disability; there are schemes for the *waiving or reduction of various charges and costs* (including medical, dental and optical charges; costs of school meals and clothing; and charges for personal social services - the last of which are covered in detail in chapter 5). Nevertheless, I trust that the above summary will leave all readers with a broad picture of the benefit context within which the discussion in this book takes place.

Something also needs to be said about the *discretionary funds* which, although they are not strictly speaking part of the benefit system, supplement or are tangled up with it to one degree or another. It is to these that we now turn.

Discretionary Funds

1. The Social Fund.

Perhaps the best-known of these discretionary funds, the Social Fund is an ambiguous phenomenon in that, while it can be advantageous in individual cases, it is on the whole more of a problem than a solution and indeed can be a considerable financial hazard to those who find themselves involved with it.

In April 1988, the old system of supplementary benefit "single payments" - grants for essential items such as household equipment, bedding and sometimes clothing - was finally abolished(swingeing preliminary cuts having been made some 20 months earlier). The Social Fund was put in its place but, compared with the position prior to the 1986 cuts, this represented a reduction in resources for grants in excess of 80 per cent, as the Social Fund, highly discretionary and cash-limited with greatly reduced appeal rights, deals largely in loans (to the extent of 70 percent of its budget). These have to be repaid by weekly reductions in benefit, taking claimants below the income support level. Thus, one problem is replaced by another - a broken cooker or worn-out mattress dealt with at the cost of a debt which is guaranteed to deepen the claimant's poverty.

The residual grant element within the Social Fund provides for "community care grants", which amongst other things are supposed to help people to remain in, or resettle into, the community. The Social Fund thus incorporates an explicit reference to the subject of this book: but the good which the grant system might do is more than offset by the hazards posed by loans. Alarmingly, even somebody already experiencing great hardship can - if only because of the state of the local office budget - apply for a grant and end up with a loan.

A great deal has been written about the Social Fund. One of the most authoritative, comprehensive and damning reports is that commissioned by the DSS itself - from the Social Policy Research Unit at York University - and published very much without fanfare. (Dix and Huby, 1992).

Some other payments, for maternity and funeral expenses and the extra fuel costs of exceptionally cold weather, come under the auspices of the Social Fund, although they really constitute a separate system, without the repayments, cash-limiting, extensive discretion and lack of appeal rights of the main fund.

2. The Family Fund.

Although Government-financed, the Family Fund has operated hitherto under the auspices of the Joseph Rowntree Foundation. It transfers to independent status in 1995. Based in York, the Family Fund has been in existence since the early 1970s, for the purpose of making lump-sum grants to help families with severely disabled children. Originally, the Family Fund was "...hastily contrived in order to prevent a parliamentary defeat for the Heath government during the political crisis over compensation to thalidomide children in late 1972". (Bradshaw and Hood, 1977). It is a modest adjunct to the social security system, operating on a fairly small scale, but generally seems to be well-regarded and nowadays un-controversial. There is no formal means test, but applicants' financial resources are taken into account in a more general sense.

3. The Independent Living Fund.

The Independent Living Fund (ILF) makes payments to help finance high-cost care packages for severely disabled people.(See Lakey, 1994; George, 1994a). It is (like the severe disability premium) a product of parliamentary concern over the loss of additional disability-related payments which could be made under the old supplementary benefit scheme. It has had a troubled history, entailing conflict between the trustees and the Government over the level of resources made available, resulting-under the new community care arrangements - in the winding up of the Fund as originally constituted. Resources have been transferred to SSDs to help them to pick up this area of work; a residual "continuation" fund has been retained to deal with the remaining caseload of the original body; and a much smaller "Independent Living (1993) Fund" has been set up. The 1993 Fund requires, in each individual case, a complicated joint financing arrangement between the Fund and the SSD. Perhaps partly because of its complexity, it has been, in its early stages, considerably under-subscribed in spite of its modest resources. The exclusion of disabled people aged 65 or over is also a major limiting factor.

The ILF does involve some degree of *direct payment* to the disabled person him or herself and this is widely welcomed by recipients. Consequently, the transfer of most of the resources to SSDs, which at the time of writing do not have powers to make payments direct to service users, has given renewed stimulus to the debate as to whether they should now be given such powers. This question is considered further in chapter 7. Whether the ILF would itself survive such a change in SSDs' powers must be questionable: there would undoubtedly be suggestions of duplication.

There are other, analogous bodies - certain charities instigated by the Government - which similarly function on the fringes of the benefit system. Motability is an example from the 1970s, a body which helps disabled people with the purchase or lease of cars; while more recently there have been various trusts connected with AIDS and HIV infection.

Having summarised the various benefits and funds and flagged up some problem areas, let us turn now to examine the way in which these feed into community care finance.

Financing the System

There is a general sense in which social security and welfare benefits underpin financially the community care programme, insofar as they make provision (however imperfectly)for a person's basic and essential needs, such as food, clothing, fuel and housing costs. This is why maximisation of uptake of benefit entitlements is very important if we are serious about enabling vulnerable people to live in the community with the greatest possible degree of independence. This theme is developed in detail in chapter 6. This is also why it is counter-productive if charges for care services are so high as to leave service users with a seriously deficient disposable income - see chapter 5.

Charges for care services indeed constitute the second sense in which benefits underlie community care policy, for charges are levied upon benefit income in both the residential and (increasingly) the domiciliary contexts. As well as examining the tension between revenue-raising and protection of service users' disposable incomes, chapter 5 will explore the confusing question of what different benefits are supposed to be "for". It will also consider the way in which charging for domiciliary and day care services is being manipulated by the Government as a device to reduce grant support to SSDs; and how the benefit entitlements of residents of care homes have been "rigged" to encourage the supplanting of LA by P&V sector provision.

In accommodation, such as supported lodgings, hostels and group homes, which lie in between the domiciliary and full residential settings, there are special questions relating to housing benefit, which are explored in chapter 4.

There are also NHS powers to provide support to community care initiatives, including joint finance agreements with SSDs and "dowries" which can subsidise accommodation of and services to people who are being resettled from long-stay hospitals. These powers can sit uneasily alongside the benefit system, causing problems for various benefit entitlements if the BA decides that the NHS should take responsibility (see chapter 4).

For our present purposes, though, I would like to look at a very specific sense in which benefits link up with community care finance. This concerns LA funding of places in residential care and nursing homes.

The "Transfer of Funds"

It would be useful at this point to remind ourselves of the way in which SSD funds and benefit income interact in the P&V residential context. As noted in chapter 2, the SSD - once having established that the care home is appropriate to the service user's needs - then has a duty to ensure that fees are paid, if such accommodation is not "otherwise available" to the resident.(The SSD is not required to take financial responsibility if the resident has sufficient resources to pay for him or herself).This means that the SSD finances the difference between the home's fees and the amount contributed by the resident through the charge levied by the SSD. The claimant is assessed for income support purposes according to the ordinary rules, except for the addition of the residential allowance, but has to contribute most of his or her income towards the cost of the care home place.

Prior to the 1993 changes, however, the DSS was responsible(subject to the various limits) for meeting care home costs for these residents. It was therefore agreed that the DSS would transfer to SSDs *the amount which it would have spent* on income support (and AA or DLAC, which used to be paid to residents along with income support) *if the old system had continued.* This amount would, though, be reduced by the amount of the DSS's extra spending on the ordinary personal allowances and premiums (which would now be payable instead of the small personal expenses allowance) and on the residential allowance. Also netted off would be the continuing, but declining, cost of benefit spending on the "preserved group" still within the old system.

The amount to be transferred had to be estimated, taking into account a number of complex variables, including demographic trends amongst the different categories of potential care home residents; the rate of diminution of the "preserved group" through death and discharge; the possible patterns of movement from one type of care to another; the hypothetical effect of future uprating of "old system" benefit limits; and the reduction in NHS continuing care provision. While this exercise was in theory a scientific statistical undertaking, strong vested interests were of course at play in the many areas where the future was far from clear. Obviously, the DSS would be seeking conservative estimates of factors which would tend to increase the transfer, while the LA Associations would have the opposite incentive (although there were exceptions to this pattern, notably the protracted wrangle over how rental costs should be met, when the different proposed solutions, reflecting various different agendas, divided the LA Associations and the central government departments amongst themselves - see chapter 2).

While highly specialised matters such as rental costs and the more esoteric statistical problems were diverted to various sub-groups and working parties, the main forum for the lengthy discussions concerning the transfer of funds was a joint central/local government committee referred to as the "Algebra Group". The name alone was enough to strike apprehension into the hearts of SSDs, which increasingly formed the view that whatever was going to happen was not going to be straightforward. As there were over three years of discussion between White Paper and implementation, there was plenty of time to become nervous.

In the event, how well or otherwise an individual SSD would do out of the transfer would depend not only on the global sum, but also on the distributional method - that is, the way in which the "cake" would be divided up. In the first year (1993/4)concern to protect the position of P&V sector homes which had been heavily reliant on income support payments led to a hybrid formula which partly employed the usual government distributional methodology based on the central view of the local need to spend(the "standard spending assessment") and partly on the existing geographical pattern of income support payments to P&V sector care home residents. In the second year, the latter element was removed. Although making more sense in terms of the objective of developing new patterns of care services, this switch in distributional methodology caused a substantial degree of instability in the budgets of a number of LAs, helping to get several county councils in particular into serious difficulties in the second year. Some adjustment to the standard spending assessment is to be made in the third year, to try to soften to at least some degree the impact of the change on the worst-affected SSDs.

The transferred funding is being phased in over three years, each year's amount being absorbed into the LA's base budget the following year. (The phasing-in period was originally to be five years, but this was curtailed, controversially and without consultation). After some debate, temporary "ring fencing" arrangements were put in place, to make sure that the money is spent on community care. All in all, the transfer, taken together with pre-existing central government grant support for LA social services; any "earmarked" funding which might be paid from time to time for particular purposes; and revenue from charges, is in theory supposed to be enough to pay for places in care homes and develop community-based alternatives. In cases where this optimism proves to be misplaced, the LA concerned can be left with little or no room for manoeuvre, as council tax "capping" severely restricts local government's ability to raise additional revenue.

Problems with Funding

Firstly, there is the question *whether or not the resources available for community care really are "enough"*. Of course, one could always find good arguments for greater resources, but a sufficiently large shortfall will undoubtedly frustrate public expectations and could stretch SSDs' ability even to fulfil their legal duties (see below). The social security transfer element, combined with an additional amount for home and respite care and the transferred ILF resources, are referred to as the "special transitional grant" (STG). For financial year 1995/6, the Government has announced figures (for England) of:

	517.7m.	(social security transfer element);
	30.0m.	(home and respite care addition);
	99.9m.	(ILF element).
Total:	647.6m.	

(Source: DoH, 1994a).

According to the AMA and ACC, this - taken together with mainstream central support for personal social services and the amounts already absorbed into baseline budgets from the previous two years - represents a substantial shortfall, compared with estimated corresponding costs. The Associations anticipate a gap between funding and necessary spending, in 1995/6, of some 863 million in terms of personal social services overall, of which 261 million is attributed to the new community care arrangements. The community care deficiency is estimated by the LA Associations to be likely to grow to around 796 million by 1997/8, on current assumptions. (ACC and AMA, 1994). (Although all of the above figures are for England, similar pressures would be found in Scotland and Wales).

While there is no doubt room for argument, a shortfall of anything like these proportions cannot but be a cause for great concern.

The reasons for this overall financial deficiency are various, but include, according to the LA Associations, a failure to provide adequately for "infrastructure costs" - including new assessment and care management systems and information technology; and an underestimation of the impact on SSD budgets of the NHS-led redefinition of the health and social care boundary (discussed in chapter 4).

Secondly, the *distribution* of the STG and of the balance of central government grant support presents a number of problems. The operation of the Revenue Support Grant and the standard spending assessment is, to put it as kindly as possible, imperfect (some would say eccentric; and some would allege political bias). This is not the place to explore this complex issue: suffice it to say that unpredictability and apparent irrationality are well-established features of these distributional mechanisms. Moreover, as noted above, this has been exacerbated in the second year of the new system by the switch in the basis of the distribution specifically of the STG. Commenting on vacillations of funding between different LAs over time, the ACC has observed succinctly that: "Social services authorities are not "losers" or "winners". The losers are the people in need of community care services". (ACC,1994).

Bizarre patterns of resource allocation between LAs, though, are not only the result of eccentric distributive effects in relation to funds transferred for community care. There is also *the interaction between resources for community care and the wider mechanisms and politics of local government finance*. In a given LA, it is perfectly possible for "extra" funding to be more than offset by cuts to the existing base (because of alleged "over-spending") so that the net effect is service cuts, in spite of ring-fencing of the "newer" resources.

Two other difficulties remain to be mentioned in relation to funding. One is the Government's *requirement that at least 85 per cent of the social security transfer element of the STG must be spent in the P&V sector*. Because this is underdeveloped in many areas as regards domiciliary and day care, a distorting effect has emerged whereby a number of SSDs are having to opt for residential care in cases where the client could be supported in the community if the money available could be spent on LA services (see e.g. AMA, 1994a; Clark, 1994). I have put it to the DoH, during consultations, that there is a conflict here between the Government's espousal of the community care approach on the one hand and its over-zealous devotion to the private sector on the other, the latter sentiment proving easily the stronger. Nor should this be seen as a party political divide, as many Conservative councillors on Social Services Committees will readily testify. Sustained pressure from LA interests has recently led to some relaxation of the "85 per cent" rule. It remains to be seen whether, when transitional finance has run its course, the Government will seek further means to manipulate the pattern of LA spending in this area.

Finally, there is the fact that *the social security transfer does not include any element to cover the shortfall between income support "old system" limits and care homes' fees*. This deficit was estimated by the LA Associations to be 66m. at the start of the new system. The Government's position was that, since the transfer was concerned with the resources which the DSS would have spent, had the old system continued, it was by definition not obliged to transfer those which - however controversially - it would not have spent. During consultations, the LA Associations sought to establish why the Government considered that this issue would not be a problem for SSDs, when it had been a major headache for the DSS. The following arguments were put forward by the DSS and DoH:

- SSDs can use their local bargaining power, conferred by their new control over care purchasing resources, to exert downward pressure on charges;

- a proportion of service users who might have gone into a care home will, under the new system, be maintained in the community, usually at lower cost;

- SSDs can, in any case, bid for compensatory extra funds as part of the normal grant aid settlement.

As Michael Hill and I have argued elsewhere (Fimister and Hill, 1993, p106) the strength of the first of these arguments will vary from one area to another, depending on the state of the local market: that is, the degree to which proprietors are dependent on SSD-supported residents; the second is no doubt true to a degree, but to what degree is not known; while the third -"you can always ask for more money, but don't count on it" - is hardly helpful, especially in the present public spending climate. The idea that the shortfall will be substantially offset by the above three factors does not, then, seem mathematically robust.

It is true that an Audit Commission survey of a third of English and Welsh LAs concluded that inadequate local financial controls played some part in the overall financial problem, along with other factors including distributional changes and high levels of demand. (Audit Commission, 1994). Nevertheless, the funding shortfall and distributional quirks described above are undoubtedly the main factors at work.

Moreover, LAs which find themselves under-resourced in terms of their community care responsibilities may well face legal challenges in endeavouring to ration services. A case is on its way through the courts at the time of writing in which one LA - Gloucestershire - faces a challenge as to the lawfulness of its decision to withdraw services on financial grounds from two clients when there had been no change in their care needs. Agencies representing the interests of community care service users are increasingly inclined to consider recourse to the law to challenge doubtful policies and practices. Indeed, the Public Law Project has published a guide to assist them to do so. (Public Law Project, 1994). Such legal challenges are also increasingly likely to be brought to bear on dubious charging practices (see chapter 5).

My own contacts with pressure groups in this field suggest that there is an appreciation of the fact that the resource problems can for the most part be laid at central government's door; but also a belief that service users' rights must nevertheless be asserted if they are not to be forgotten. There is tied up in this a hope that high-profile legal cases will indirectly put pressure on central government to enhance resources. There is of course the danger that the Government will instead act to dilute rights, but this would be politically controversial and it seems more likely that the existing tension between rights to services and inadequate resources will be allowed to continue.

This chapter has endeavoured to describe the bewildering variety of different benefits and funding mechanisms. In the next, I shall go on to describe how these cluster together around different types of supported accommodation.

Chapter 4

A Typology of Accommodation

Summary

Although care needs can be seen as a finely-graded continuum, ranging from relatively modest domiciliary support through various forms of supported accommodation to care in a nursing home or hospital, the benefit and charging rules seek to dispense with subtle shading and put service users into separate boxes governed by different sets of rules. This can look arbitrary and confusing in the real world.

This chapter begins by considering the "frontier" between hospital treatment and care in the nursing home sector, summarising the controversy which has developed around this question. It then goes on to set out a "typology" of benefit and charging regimes in different types of supported accommodation: that provided by LAs where board is included and where it is not; and that provided in the P&V sector, registered and unregistered.("Supported" accommodation in this context means homes, hostels and other settings where personal care and/ or counselling and other support is provided, ranging from residential care and nursing homes to supported lodgings). Issues and problems are discussed and the chapter ends with a close look at the role of HB and the "registration" controversy.

Readers should note that the systems and structures considered in this chapter are particularly likely to prove liable to change. Current specialist advice should always be taken when planning services or advising service users and carers.

NHS Patient or Community Care Service User?

Before considering further the benefit and charging issues around the different types of supported accommodation which are to be found within the community care field, something needs to be said about the lack of clarity as to whether some service users ought more properly to be regarded as NHS patients. This is important, as hospital care under the NHS is free at the point of access (although benefits are reduced - "downrated" - by various amounts at different stages); whereas residential or nursing home care under LA auspices involves charging (while most - although not all - benefits are unchanged: see chapter 3 for more detail).

If the Benefits Agency thinks that the circumstances are such that the NHS has responsibility for a particular person, then he or she may be treated by the BA as a hospital patient, even if in accommodation which purports not to be a hospital. NHS hospital patients receive much lower benefits than they otherwise would, because of the above-mentioned "hospital downrating" rules. Categorisation as a hospital patient for benefit purposes depends on whether or not a person is held by the BA to be receiving free treatment as an in-patient in a hospital "or similar institution". A "similar institution" is not defined in the legislation, so there is room for argument and ambiguity.

The BA will be especially suspicious where a health authority or trust has been closely involved in the setting up of the establishment concerned. Collaborative LA/NHS initiatives involving joint finance, sometimes on former NHS sites and with a variety of staffing arrangements, can involve a high degree of unpredictability in terms of the benefit status of residents. The matter can be complicated further by inconsistent decisions between different parts of the BA. For example, advisers report that sometimes a local BA office will decide that a person is not a hospital patient, while the central AA/DLA unit takes the contrary view. Readers experiencing difficulty in this general area should seek specialist welfare rights advice, including as regards the current state of play in relation to case law (precedent-setting decisions of the courts and Social Security Commissioners).

"Hospital patient" status will sometimes leave the service user with more and sometimes with less income than they would have with standard LA personal expenses allowances (the amount left after paying LA charges).

A further factor is that there is, as a hospital patient, no means-testing of capital assets in order to meet the costs of accommodation and care. On the other hand, some projects for less dependent residents (typically younger people with disabilities) permit the retention of much higher personal expenses allowances than the standard amount (see below); and some supported accommodation schemes may genuinely depend for their survival on levying charges on higher rates of benefit - so the position is complex as regards the balance of residents' interests. This is not a new problem: it applied under the pre-April 1993 system, with even higher amounts of benefit at stake under the old nursing home formula for income support.

A particular aspect of the "frontier" between NHS and LA care which has often caused difficulty to service users and their families, as well as to SSDs and their budgets, has been the phenomenon whereby very highly dependent people have been discharged from NHS care into the LA means-tested system, when they should have continued to receive care free at the point of access under the NHS. It was clear in the latter years of the "old" (pre-April 1993) system that the problem of such discharges, especially into private nursing homes, was increasing. It was, moreover, particularly serious given the income support "limits" (which of course still apply to the "preserved" group) as relatives, often themselves elderly, could face severe financial hardship in trying to meet the shortfall. There were allegations, also, that NHS personnel misled patients and relatives into believing that they had no choice but to agree to discharge and a private nursing home; and that misleadingly optimistic accounts were given as to the availability of income support. (See, for example, Age Concern, 1989; or the Alzheimer's Disease Society quoted in House of Commons Health Committee, 1993, para. 35).

In theory, relatives' hardship in these circumstances should be mitigated under the new system in that SSDs cannot lawfully impose arbitrary limits on the charges that they will meet: if the care is needed, it should be provided to at least an adequate level in one form or another. Nevertheless, even without these limits, charging can - and in an unknown number of cases does - cause hardship to partners of people in care homes. This is discussed further in chapter 5. Moreover, the problem of arbitrary limits does not, in practice, seem to have been banished: enquiries to pressure groups and welfare rights advisers suggest that some LAs are exerting pressure for "third party" contributions to the cost of a place in a particular home without being able to demonstrate - as the law requires - that a cheaper suitable alternative is in fact on offer.

Pressure to clear beds and reduce waiting lists has been building up within the NHS for a number of years. This is exacerbated by the new market ethos, which serves to encourage the off loading of financially burdensome responsibilities. In this context, the broad nature of SSDs' duties to pay for care home places creates a clear danger of "dumping" by health authorities and trusts. To prevent (or at least phase) this, the DoH has repeatedly stressed the need for local consultation and orderly transition. This has not, though, prevented the question of responsibilities from becoming very much a live political issue. In June 1993, the House of Commons Health Committee (1993, para. 37) recommended that service users should be "...given a full opportunity to exercise choice about their destination after hospital without being subject to undue pressure". Organisations representing the interests of service users and of their informal carers continued to express concern. Then, in February 1994, the Health Service Commissioner (Ombudsman) reported on the case of a patient discharged by Leeds Health Authority (now called "Leeds Healthcare") in spite of still needing intensive nursing care following a stroke. Caught by the "old system" income support limits, his wife had to pay 12,000 over two years towards private nursing home fees. Although compensation was duly paid in this case (following the Ombudsman's intervention) the latter, Mr. William Reid, was subsequently quoted as observing that "...the case was probably one of many throughout the country in which health authorities were failing in their duty to provide adequate after care for disabled patients". (Wright, 1994; see also Brindle, 1994a; and Burgess, 1994).

In the wake of this case, the Ombudsman's office was "...inundated with inquiries from families in similar positions". (Brindle, 1994b). A survey of 80 LAs conducted by the Labour Party was subsequently reported as finding that "about one quarter...had terminally ill patients dumped on them by hospitals. Half of the councils said the NHS was shifting costs onto them. One respondent said: "Of all community care placements in nursing homes (mainly from hospital discharge) 9 per cent have died in four weeks and 16 per cent have died in eight weeks". (News item, Community Care, 15-21.12.94, p1).

The furore over the Leeds and similar cases intensified the pressure on the DoH to take steps to clarify the matter. However, provisional guidance, when it arrived (issued as a draft - NHS Executive, 1994), was imprecise and evasive. For example (on p.2): "Health Authorities and GP Fundholders should determine, in close consultation with local social services departments, the level, type and range of services which they should purchase in the light of local circumstances...... Different models of care may be appropriate in different parts of the country". Such confusing generalisations might be thought to reflect the political need to fudge the contradictions between legal duties and market orientation within the NHS. Even so, the guidance gave enough of a green light to means-testing in the nursing context to have led to questions about the lawfulness of the advice in terms of health legislation. (Clements, 1994).

Sensitive to the continuing controversy, especially in the context of the growing crisis over community care funding in many parts of the country (see chapter 3), the revised version of the guidance produced by the DoH in March of 1995 was much more detailed (DoH, 1995). It continued to emphasise local agreements, but stated prominently that (para. 1): "The arrangement and funding of services to meet continuing physical and mental health care needs are an integral part of the responsibilities of the NHS"; and stressed that (para. 3): "health authorities and GP Fundholders failing currently to arrange and fund a full range of services (are required) to make the necessary investment in their 1996/7 contracts to address this".

Such statements sound forthright and are certainly helpful as far as they go. The "small print", though, leaves cause for concern. Local variation is still espoused - which can be seen as a practical reflection of the real world, or as a means of obscuring the overall funding picture. Health authorities are expected to agree their "purchasing decisions" with LAs "if possible" (annex A, para. A) - which again could be merely practical common sense, or anticipation of continuing cause for LA concern. Health authorities and GP Fundholders "will need to set priorities for continuing health care within the total resources available to them" (para. 12) - a phrase with a special meaning in the context of cash-limited and devolved budgets (that is, "if the money isn't enough, blame your own budget management skills, not the Government"). Thus, the financial pressures and vested interests which have caused the current dispute over responsibilities continue to rumble underneath the new guidance. There is no doubt that we have not heard the last of this issue.

Supported Accommodation: A Typology

As noted in chapter 2, there is not a simple dichotomy between residential care and ordinary housing: there is a continuum, with a variety of types of accommodation ranged between the extremes of high and low "dependency". The benefit and charging systems, though, do not reflect the gradual nature of this continuum: they leap dramatically from one regime to another, amongst residents whose circumstances are often quite similar. Service users, their relatives and carers are of course frequently baffled by this, as are the staff of social services, health and housing agencies, which do not necessarily have ready access to specialist interpretation of these strange goings-on.

Thus, as the benefit changes in relation to supported lodgings, hostels and "small homes" pursued their convoluted course (see chapter 2) and the 1993 changes to the funding of residential care and nursing home places appeared on the horizon, one of the most frequent requests to emerge from the "front line" was for a simple typology of the different benefit and charging regimes which applied to different sorts of accommodation. Alas, there are limits to how far the fundamentally convoluted can be represented in a simple fashion, but such a typology was produced and has been published in various places (see e.g. Fimister, 1993 and 1993b). The following account elaborates on this and brings it up to date. I must, however, sound a note of caution. There are several reasons why a given real-life situation may not appear to fit into the typology. These can be summarised as:

Exceptions to rules: There are some specialised contexts, including hospices, Abbeyfield Homes and places provided under certain mental health legislation where variations apply;

Transitional arrangements: When there is a change to benefit provision, existing cases usually have some form of limited protection, which may last for some years and become increasingly mysterious as memories of the old rules fade;

Temporary payments: Some benefits will continue in payment for short periods when circumstances change - for example, AA and DLAC are normally paid for 28 days after admission to a residential care or nursing home;

Unclear legislation: Notably in relation to AA and DLAC, where confusion around responsibility for care and accommodation costs (discussed in chapter 3 and earlier in this chapter) can lead to the award and refusal of benefit to different claimants in very similar circumstances - indeed, even in the same accommodation. (The outcomes of AA and DLAC claims are so unpredictable in some parts of the country that one social worker simply refused to believe me that they were not discretionary payments, like the Social Fund);

Inconsistent adjudication: Which can arise from unclear legislation, but which also derives from...

Local variation in interpretation of the rules: For example, levels of HB can vary very greatly because of differing treatment of service charges, especially for general counselling and support; and SSDs vary greatly in the extent to which they use their discretionary powers in relation to charging for residential accommodation (see chapter 5). Some variations result from unawareness amongst officers of the agencies concerned of aspects of the relevant law. Some variations result from unlawful policies or practices: for example, a number of HB authorities never pay benefit above the level which the rent officer authorises for subsidy, even though the law requires that each case should be looked at on its merits and (until October 1995, when the Government intends to remove this protection)specifically exempts certain "vulnerable" claimants from such restriction. Unlawful practices usually arise from a failure to take competent - or indeed, any - legal advice about complex legislation;

Administrative error: An anomalous-looking benefit or charging arrangement can arise because the BA, HB authority or SSD has simply made a mistake - there is plenty of scope for error and confusion in this field. Sometimes, the error will be caused by failure on the service user's part to provide full or correct information or to notify a change of circumstances: again, the complexity of the system often engenders confusion as to what information is required and when.

It can be difficult to tell which of the above factors is at work. For example, three young people with learning disabilities live in registered supported lodgings. Two of them have the residential allowance included within their income support; the other receives HB. The HB authority might have made a mistake (as HB is not payable in respect of registered accommodation) or might not have identified the claim as relating to registered premises.

Or our third resident may have transitional protection from the pre-April 1993 rules, when HB could be paid.

Bearing in mind all of the above caveats, it is possible to divide supported accommodation into four broad types for benefit and charging purposes. The DoH and DSS have attempted, in developing charging and benefit systems, to distinguish between "more dependent" and "less dependent" residents. In LA accommodation (by which I mean that which is provided directly by the SSD) the provision of board marks the boundary: if board is provided, then situation A below applies; while if it is not, benefits and charges are as per situation B. (The definition of "board" is considered later in this chapter). This distinction is the result of pressure from the LA Associations to protect the position of certain LA projects, notably for younger disabled people, which were brought for the first time within the ambit of Part 111 of the 1948 National Assistance Act by the 1990 legislation. Without criteria to separate it off, this accommodation would from April 1993 have fallen within the highly restrictive rules applying to care homes for dependent elderly people, leaving the residents with minimal disposable incomes and costing SSDs an additional financial outlay in making up lost HB. While co-operating with the LA Associations' wishes to avoid these consequences, the DSS nevertheless was quick to take steps, in the run-up to the 1993 changes, to prevent SSDs from switching existing "Part 111" residents to the more favourable regime by ceasing to provide board. Some SSDs had begun to do just this, although they protested that the promotion of greater independence for the resident, rather than the financial attraction of transferring costs to HB, had been their motivation.

In the P&V sector, registration with the local or health authority as a care or nursing home marks the boundary between situation C ("more dependent") and D ("less dependent"). I have already described, in chapter 2, how this change (effective from April 1993) was bulldozed through by the DSS in place of the former "care test".

Although the board and registration tests are intended to distinguish different categories of "dependency", these are clearly very blunt instruments. The wide and indiscriminate effects of the registration test on supported lodgings and similar provision is the obvious example, but there will be many other cases where a "less dependent" resident will fall under a "more dependent" accommodation heading. The areas of discretion in relation to charging which are referred to below and in chapter 5 should therefore be kept very much in mind. (Chapter 5 also questions the adequacy of the standard personal expenses allowance even for "more dependent" residents).

If we combine the LA and P&V sectors with the board and registration tests, we have four different benefit and charging scenarios, as follows:

A: LA accommodation - board provided.

The LA residential accommodation rate of income support applies. HB is not payable; nor are AA and DLAC (even if the resident is paying the full cost of the place). The claimant will normally retain only the small standard personal expenses allowance after the charge has been levied (although there are powers to pay more in exceptional circumstances - see chapter 5).

B: LA accommodation - board not provided.

Ordinary income support entitlements apply. HB is payable but AA and DLAC are not (again, even if the resident is paying the full cost of the place). The LA is expected to use its powers to permit a significantly higher disposable income than at A after the charge has been levied (see chapter 5 for a more detailed discussion of this point).

C: P&V sector accommodation - registered.

Ordinary income support entitlements apply, except for the addition of the residential allowance. HB is not payable. AA and DLAC are generally not payable, unless there is no LA involvement in financing the accommodation (a "loophole" which the DSS may move to close). If the SSD is financially involved in this way, not only are AA/DLAC lost, but the claimant will normally retain only the small standard personal expenses allowance after the charge has been levied, unless (as at A above) the SSD uses its discretion to allow more. (Note that it is the SSD's involvement in paying for accommodation -including for services which are an integral part of the accommodation charge- which causes AA and DLAC to be lost: SSD provision of other services ought not to be a problem).

D: P&V sector accommodation - not registered.

For the sake of simplicity, I shall assume here that the SSD is not contributing towards the cost of the accommodation. (The extent and nature of SSDs' powers to finance placements in unregistered P&V sector accommodation is the subject of some confusion at the time of writing, the legislation being fragmented and interpretation debatable).

Ordinary income support entitlements apply and HB is payable. AA and DLAC should be payable (although there may be problems in practice). The claimant's disposable income, after the accommodation charge has been paid, should be significantly higher than at C, assuming that the proprietor is not charging too close to the resident's total income.

It can be seen from the above that higher disposable incomes and payment of HB are features of those scenarios in which residents are expected to live more independent lives, closer to the mainstream of community life in general than is possible for those with greater ill-health or disability. The issues around charging and disposable incomes are explored in chapter 5; those around the role of HB are discussed below.

Housing Benefit and Community Care

I referred briefly in chapter 3 to the importance of HB to people on low incomes. For all its imperfections, there is no doubt that poverty would cut far deeper without it. It is for this reason that the steady erosion of HB through steepening of withdrawal rates, increase in assumed contributions from "non-dependants" and subsidy reductions to LAs has been such a cause for concern. In spite of cuts in the "generosity" of the scheme, its cost has continued to rise, partly because of claimant numbers (particularly as a result of high unemployment)but - as the government admits - "...the increase (arises) primarily from real increases in the level of rents in all parts of the rented housing market". (DSS, 1993, para. 4.7).

These rent increases are, moreover, a direct result of Government housing market policies: decontrol within the private sector and large-scale cuts in subsidy within the LA and, increasingly, the housing association sectors, have led to a quite deliberate pattern of rent rises all round. The Department of the Environment originally defended this by arguing that it was preferable for subsidy to be concentrated on needy individuals through the

HB scheme. DSS ministers then took to complaining that HB was extending further up the income scale and increasing in cost (both of which effects follow naturally from rent rises) and should therefore be cut. Here is a striking example of policy conflict between Departments producing nonsensical results.

As noted in chapter 3, the DSS - as part of the Government's continuing review of the benefit system - has recently announced further cuts in HB, due to take effect in October 1995, in the private deregulated rented sector. Housing associations will also be affected if the HB authority chooses to exercise its discretion in such cases to refer the rent to the Rent Officer Service for a determination of the amount of central government HB subsidy (see below and chapter 3 as regards the role of rent officers). The latter problem will especially be an issue where the HB authority is not the same as the social services authority - see below.

Meanwhile, a broader debate is opening up, within and outside the Government, concerning the deleterious effects of a "high rents" policy on employment strategies and on the wider economy (see Meen, 1994; Wilcox, 1994). We cannot pursue this important debate here: suffice it to say that its outcome could have a significant bearing on the well being of millions of people on low incomes, including large numbers of community care clients.

Aside from the general importance of HB, there are more specific reasons for its significance to community care provision. I noted in chapter 3 that, although HB cannot be paid in respect of charges for personal care, it can in certain circumstances meet the costs of general counselling and support. Although these are normally ineligible for HB, they can be met where the landlord, landlady or their employees who provide the counselling and support spend more than half of their time also providing other services which are eligible (that is, those which are more directly related to the provision of housing, as specified in the HB regulations). The "50 per cent rule", as it has come to be known, is a helpful and constructive tie-in between housing, social security and community care policies which is important to the functioning of a number of hostels, supported lodgings and similar projects. Its operation, however, is not trouble-free. There is considerable local variation in the way that HB authorities interpret the rules, leading to widely varying levels of HB. Linked to this is wide local variation in the way that rent officers approach the determination of the amounts eligible for subsidy. (Rent officers are effectively independent of

LAs and - as noted in chapter 3 -are responsible for determining the amount of subsidy, in relation to most private sector rents, which is payable by the DSS to the HB authority. They can also consider housing association rents if referred by the HB authority). Moreover, in those areas which are not covered by single-tier LAs, the HB and social services authorities are at separate tiers, which has sometimes led to friction, as the policies of county SSDs (and their Scottish counterparts) in pursuit of their community care responsibilities have caused district HB authorities to incur costs in making up subsidy shortfalls.

In late 1994, the DSS commissioned research (from the Social Policy Research Unit at York University) into service charges and how they are dealt with within the HB scheme. This includes the operation of the "50 per cent rule". Results are expected during 1995. It is to be hoped that any changes consequent upon this will clarify and consolidate, rather than weaken or remove, this valuable provision. It is also to be hoped that the proposed October 1995 cuts will not impact upon these or other service charges - something which is still under discussion at the time of writing.

Readers of this book may wish to note that research is also currently under way, financed by the Joseph Rowntree Foundation and conducted by Steve Griffiths, under the working title of How Housing Benefit Can Work for Community Care. It is hoped that this, too, will be published during 1995. Amongst other topics, it covers the issues around the "50 per cent rule" and the very difficult problems caused by the registration test, to which we now turn.

The Registration Test

As noted in chapter 2, when the DSS announced its intention to utilise, from April 1993, the new registration requirement in respect of "small homes" as the determinant of whether or not HB was payable, the LA Associations were at pains to explain that this would draw many projects into the "high dependency" benefit and charging regime (C above) which ought not to be there. The DSS remained unmoved, even after the policy consequences for community care had been fully explained, detailed exemplifications provided and a simplified version of the previous "care test" put forward as an alternative.

Claimants resident at the point of change were to have transitional protection: that is, they could continue to receive HB as long as they remained in the same accommodation. New claimants, though, would instead have the residential allowance added to their income support requirements. Although in some cases the residential allowance might not be greatly different to the HB which would have been payable under the old system, it would be considerably less where general counselling and support which would formerly have been covered by HB under the "50 per cent rule" was at all substantial. This shortfall would frequently require the SSD to step in with financial support under its 1948 National Assistance Act powers (assuming it thought the care appropriate and the cost acceptable compared with possible alternatives) which would lead the BA to withdraw AA or DLAC, which would in turn knock out any income support severe disability premium which was payable. (The scale of the problem in any given instance would of course depend on the nature and degree of the resident's disability and the precise combination of benefits consequently in payment). This "domino effect" has indeed subsequently befallen small-scale, supported accommodation up and down the country. Not only do such cases require a substantial financial contribution from the SSD, but they also draw residents into the latter's charging system. Unless the SSD exercises its discretion to permit a personal expenses allowance greater than normal (which it would obviously have to subsidise through revenue forgone) the service user is left with a disposable income of only 13-35 per week (1995/6 rates) - a hopeless basis from which to try to develop greater independence in the community.

The following example, updated from a circular which I drafted for the AMA (AMA, 1993), illustrates the position. All figures are constant at 1995/6 rates (that is, like is compared with like). The example is of a 40-year-old resident with learning disability, who has moved into supported lodgings which used to attract HB (but are now registered) and where there was no financial involvement on the part of the SSD under the old system. The accommodation is outside London and the charge is 240-00 per week.

Comparison between (weekly):

Resident's income	Old system (pre-April 1993)	New system
Severe disablement allowance plus income support:	£101-35 (inc. severe disability premium)	117-30 (inc. residential allowance)
HB:	£148-00	nil
DLAC (middle rate):	£31-20	nil
Total benefit income:	£280-55	£117-30
Cost to SSD:	nil	£136-05 (net of amount contributed by resident)
Resident's disposable income after paying charge:	£40-55	£13-35*

> * Unless the SSD exercises its discretion to allow a larger amount, in which case the "cost to SSD" figure increases correspondingly as the amount contributed by the resident reduces.

It should be noted that, in the supported lodgings context, a switch to LA funding can also have implications for the landlord/lady's own tax, national insurance contribution and benefit position (which could of course affect his or her enthusiasm for the role). Specialist advice should be sought by anybody experiencing difficulty in this area.

Given the adverse financial consequences of registration, supported accommodation projects and SSDs alike have been scrutinising very carefully the question of whether or not the accommodation concerned really has to be registered. Registration is necessary if both board and personal care are provided. If only personal care, or only board, or neither, is provided, then registration is not required. As regards personal care, neither the registration nor the social security legislation provides a clear definition, so - as in the HB scheme - the boundary between personal care and support and counselling is open to varying interpretation. Case law is beginning to develop, though, around the registration legislation, the Court of Appeal (in Harrison v. Cornwall County Council, 25.7.91) having adopted a wide-ranging approach to what is included within the scope of "personal care".

As regards board, there is again no clear definition within the registration legislation. There are, though, definitions of "board" both within charging and within benefit regulations, which establish that the charge for meals provided must be an integral part of the standard charge for the accommodation and that "pay-as-you-eat" and self-catering arrangements do not constitute board. Registration officers are not bound by charging or benefit regulations, but this approach can be urged as a model.

The matter is further complicated by the fact that, for good reasons relating to the need to exercise independent judgement, registration officers are expected to function at "arm's length" from the SSD. They therefore vary in the degree to which they are prepared to worry about the financial consequences of their decisions. As the AMA circular puts it: "Where a project provides both board and personal care, then registration is clearly required. However, it would obviously make financial sense for SSDs to invite registration officers to consider carefully in each case whether registration is really necessary, bearing in mind the factors described...above. Good liaison between finance staff, registration officers, welfare rights advisers and service providers will be important". (AMA, 1993, section 6). Not all registration officers have seen it that way, hence the wide variation in practice and consequently in projects', proprietors' and residents' finances. Frustratingly, because of the DSS's insistence on its separate agenda, combined with the DoH's refusal to get involved, registration - which, although imposing few requirements in the case of "small homes", is nevertheless supposed to be "a good thing" - has become a financial menace, jeopardising the purpose and (if the SSD will not pay) the viability of accommodation the standards of which it was intended to enhance.

Attempts to develop a rational approach to different types of accommodation and different degrees of dependency have thus foundered, yet again, on the tangled complexity of the benefit system and the conflicting policy objectives of different central government departments.

I have, moreover, touched several times in this chapter on the question of the charges levied by local government for services provided. Charges are of growing importance to SSDs in terms of revenue raised; while to the service user, the level of charge can be at least as significant, in terms of quality of life, as the level of benefit income. In the next chapter, I shall look at charges more closely.

Chapter 5

Charging for Services

Summary

This chapter explores the various issues surrounding charging for care services - in both the residential and non-residential contexts - with particular reference to their implications in terms of the benefit system. (See chapter 4 for a discussion of the controversy around the "frontier" between these services and the NHS). In the process, the growing tension is examined between the protection of service users' disposable incomes and the raising of revenue towards the cost of services. Also examined is the Government's manipulation of charging structures for wider political purposes: the promotion of the non-LA sector in residential care; and the transfer of costs from central government to service users in the non-residential field. The question is explored of what certain key benefits are "for". The chapter concludes by asking whether SSDs can reconcile these various tensions and contradictions.

Charging Frameworks

SSDs' powers and duties as regards charging for residential and nursing home places are largely set out in regulations made under the 1948 National Assistance Act, as amended by the 1990 NHS and Community Care Act. The regulations are extremely detailed, being modelled closely on the income support rules. SSDs do not have a lot of discretion in this area: but they do have some, notably in their powers to allow higher personal expenses allowances in certain circumstances and in their treatment of a resident's former home where this constitutes a capital asset. (These points are discussed further below). The LA Associations fought hard for this flexibility - through consultations with the DoH and DSS, Parliamentary lobbying and the encouragement of media coverage - so it is disappointing to note how often SSDs and/or individual members of their staff appear not to be aware of their powers in this respect.

SSDs are not legally required to charge for domiciliary and day care services, but there is considerable and growing financial pressure on them to do so. Their powers in this respect allow wide-ranging discretion in the design of charging structures. There are, nevertheless, certain legal constraints on what is permissible and it is again a cause for concern that awareness of these is often not as it should be. Powers to charge for these services are constituted under several pieces of legislation, including the Health Services and Public Health Act 1968 (in relation to the welfare of elderly people) and the National Assistance Act 1948 (in relation to the welfare of disabled people); and embrace the list of services in section 2(1) of the Chronically Sick and Disabled Persons Act 1970. Certain conditions relating to the exercise of these charging powers are imposed by the Health and Social Services and Social Security Adjudications Act 1983 (HASSASSA).

SSDs have no powers, at the time of writing, to charge for services (residential or otherwise) provided under section 117 of the Mental Health Act 1983. This seems to be an accidental inconsistency given the current policy approach, but one which -in the present climate of controversy around charging - the Government has not hastened to iron out.

Official guidance as regards charging in relation to residential and nursing home care is contained in the Charging for Residential Accommodation Guide (CRAG) (DoH & Welsh Office, 1992), a loose-leaf publication which is periodically updated. SSDs are expected to follow this. There is no official guidance in respect of domiciliary and day care charges, but the DoH has prepared an advice note, Discretionary Charges for Adult Social Services (DoH, 1994b), for the use of its Social Services Inspectorate (SSI). This has no formal status in relation to SSDs' decisions: they are not bound to follow it, although of course they must still address the legal issues which it discusses. The Commission on Social Justice (1994, p300) has called for official guidance to be introduced in respect of charging for domiciliary and day care services, but DoH ambivalence over some of the issues around charging (see below) - reflected in the advice note for the SSI - leads one to doubt the usefulness of this in the absence of a wider review of the funding structure.

It should also be said that confusion is sometimes caused around questions both of charging powers and of benefit eligibility by the fact that SSDs are often not aware of what specific legislation they are acting under in providing or financing this or that project or service. The precise powers concerned can in some cases make a difference to whether or not charges can lawfully be levied and to whether or not AA or DLAC are payable. This is a complex area where detailed specialist advice should be sought in cases of difficulty.

Residential Care and Nursing Homes

Some mention of the charging system for residential care and nursing homes has already been made in chapters 2 and 3, as an understanding of this process is important to an appreciation of both the historical and financial dimensions of community care.

Where a person is a resident of a local authority care home, the SSD is obviously able to charge that individual direct. (We shall assume for the moment that the resident is a single person: the position of couples is dealt with later in this chapter). The situation is more complex when the SSD is supporting somebody in a P&V sector home. In effect, the SSD pays the proprietor for the place and recoups as much of the cost as the rules permit from the resident by way of a charge. However, if all parties agree, the SSD can calculate the resident's contribution and leave that part of the payment to be made as a transaction between him or her and the care home, the SSD paying to the home only its own "share" of the cost. The SSD remains legally liable, though, for guaranteeing full payment to the proprietor, including making good any arrears arising from default by the resident (whom the SSD, not the proprietor, would then have to consider pursuing for repayment).

For essentially ideological reasons, the Government has, as noted in chapter 2, been keen to encourage the use of non-LA homes and correspondingly discourage authorities' use of their own provision. The structure of claimants' benefits is therefore different within the different sectors. Again as described in chapter 2, benefit levels for residents of LA homes are based on the standard retirement pension, whereas people resident in P&V sector homes are assessed under the mainstream income support system plus the additional income support residential allowance. The example below shows how the resultant higher benefits for P&V sector residents feed into higher revenue from charges.

Residential Care Homes: How the Charging Penalty Works

Example: 80-year-old resident receiving basic retirement pension. All benefits at 1995/6 rates. Lives outside Greater London (residential allowance is 6-00 higher in Greater London so penalty for LA provision would be more severe by that amount). Assumed that SSD is not using its discretion to permit the resident a higher personal expenses allowance for any reason.

P&V Sector Home		LA Home	
A. Retirement pension:	£58-85	A. Retirement pension:	£58-85
B. Income support (to bring ret. pens. up to income support level for basic living costs):	£12-80	B. Charge (A. minus 13-35 kept by resident):	£45-50
C. Income support residential allowance:	£51-00		
D. Total weekly benefit:	£122-65		
E. Charge (D. minus 13-35 kept by resident):	£109-30		

Penalty to LA for using own home:　£109-30 (charge in P&V sector home)

-£45-50 (charge in LA home)

=63-80 per resident per week

The financial incentive to place people in P&V sector homes, both before April 1993 via the special rates of supplementary benefit/income support and since that date via the above mechanism, has brought about a large-scale reduction, through closures and transfers, in provision of LA homes. This consequence has varied around the country, depending on a combination of factors including the political complexion of the LA, its overall financial position and the level of demand for care home places.

The P&V sector care home fee from which the charge to the resident is derived should be guaranteed in full by the SSD if it is agreed that the particular home represents the appropriate form of care: there should be no arbitrary limits above which the SSD will not pay (although as noted in chapter 4, these do appear to operate, unlawfully, in some areas). There are various rules to secure a degree of choice of home on the part of the service user; and to permit "top-up" payments by third parties where the SSD can legitimately hold that the resident has chosen a place which is more expensive than an adequate available alternative. (The SSD is still liable for the full cost of the place if the third party defaults, but could then revert to offering a cheaper suitable alternative as well as possibly pursuing the third party for the arrears).

In assessing the resident's contribution to the charge for a place in a residential care home (in either the LA or the P&V sector) or in a nursing home, the SSD must use the definitions of reckonable income and capital which are set out in the regulations. (Except for the first eight weeks, when there is discretion to take a different approach: see "respite and other temporary care", below). These are, as noted above, largely aligned with the income support regulations, but with certain important areas of discretion. One of these concerns the power of the SSD to disregard the value of the resident's former owner-occupied home in the community, in circumstances where somebody else is still living there. The SSD must do this, as in the income support rules, where the latter person is the care home resident's partner or a dependant aged less than 16 or an elderly or incapacitated relative. It has, moreover, a discretion to do so in other circumstances. This is intended to protect the position of, for example, an elderly companion who is not a relative; or a former live-in carer.

Disposable Incomes left to Residents

The personal expenses allowance (PEA) is the amount which should remain to a care home resident after paying the charge as determined under the charging system described above. The standard PEA at 1995/6 rates is 13-35 per week. (I shall discuss below departures from the standard amount in the cases of "less dependent" residents and in certain other circumstances). This is intended to permit a degree of personal spending on items other than those included in the charge. Having some money to spend on entertainments, maintaining social contacts, books, newspapers, personal toiletries, presents for family and friends and so on, is obviously important if the intention is to maximise quality of life and avoid mere dull and sterile institutionalisation. The PEA is also supposed to permit the purchase of replacement clothing.

A moment's thought will suggest that the level of the standard PEA is inadequate to the above task and we should be concerned at the very limited possibilities that are available to so many of our fellow citizens as a consequence of this minimalist interpretation of their personal financial needs. (A survey by Becker and colleagues, of former psychiatric patients now in residential care homes, provides interesting and disturbing evidence on the restricted lifestyles which the standard PEA imposes: see Becker, Walsh and Warden, 1990).

It should be noted, moreover, that it cannot be taken for granted that residents will receive even the inadequate amount referred to above, as in the private sector, many care home proprietors siphon off the PEA as extra revenue. This frequently occurred under the pre-April 1993 system, where fees increasingly exceeded the DSS limits and residents were often expected by proprietors to hand over the PEA to reduce the shortfall. This is still a feature of the "preserved group" arrangements. It is not, however, supposed to happen under the new system, where the SSD is intended to negotiate a fee with the proprietor and charge the resident in such a way as to provide for at least the standard PEA. Nevertheless, reports from various parts of the country suggest that many proprietors still regard the PEA as fair game and are contriving to find "extras" such as basic toilet requirements and laundry which miraculously happen to cost just this amount. I have been told by advisers working in this field that some SSDs connive in this in order to narrow down the costs included in their contracts with homes; and that some homes do not even charge for these "extras" on the basis of individual accounts, but absorb the PEA as a contribution to all residents' needs for such items.

It may at times be debatable as to what constitutes an "extra" and what is part of the care and accommodation needs which should be included in the SSD's contract with the home. The narrower the focus of the contract, though, the more likely it is that the resident will be left in a state of penniless institutionalisation. Contracts should be designed to avoid this. They should also be specific enough to avoid ambiguity as to what is covered and what is not. Proprietors who charge the resident again for items which are in the contract are of course acting fraudulently. As the Director of Social Work for Borders Regional Council in Scotland put it: "Residents should have a personal allowance to do with what they want.

It should not be used to buy care which is already paid for". (Quoted by Mitchell, 1993, p.3). Advice to SSDs on how to use their contract specifications to prevent abuse in relation to personal expenses is contained in guidance on contracting produced by the ACC, AMA and Association of Directors of Social Services (1994, pp 21-2 and 33).

Proprietors who aim to maintain high standards will frown upon practices such as those described above, although it is depressing to report that I have found confiscation of the PEA operating at the respectable end of the private care home continuum as well as at the other extreme where general standards are lower.

SSDs, as noted above, have the power to increase PEAs: that is, permit residents to retain more of their income in certain circumstances. Unless a resident is defined as "less dependent" (see below) such circumstances are supposed to be "exceptional". Higher residual incomes have in any case to be paid for by the SSD via reduced revenue from charges, so this power cannot be regarded as a universal solution to the problem of inadequacy described above. However, it can play an important role in some cases. An example would be the situation where a resident has extra expenses relating to a hobby; or where the stay in the home is expected to be temporary and the resident has continuing "outside" financial commitments such as payment instalments for essential furniture or household equipment.

There is similar protection in respect of the housing-related outside commitments of temporary residents, including rent or mortgage payments not covered by HB or income support, and items such as service charges, fixed heating charges and water rates. This protection is "to the extent that the local authority consider... reasonable in the circumstances". It is achieved not by increasing the PEA, but by disregarding an appropriate amount of income when calculating the charge.

In practice, as regards temporary residents, the SSD will often use its option not to conduct a full financial assessment during the first eight weeks, thus avoiding the process altogether for shorter breaks: see "respite and other temporary care", below.

Where residents are classed as "less dependent" (defined as living in LA residential accommodation which does not provide board or in P&V sector accommodation which is not registered) SSDs are expected to allow a greater disposable income after charging than would be the case under the standard rules. They have wide-ranging powers to depart from the latter in such cases (see the CRAG, section 2: DoH and Welsh Office, 1992). As regards "less dependent" people who do not fit that formal definition, SSDs can use their power to increase the PEA in exceptional circumstances. This latter provision will be important, for example, in respect of those people trying to live a relatively independent life in small-scale supported accommodation which has, since April 1993, been hit by the "registration test" (see chapter 4). The assumption is that less dependent, usually younger, residents will need greater spending power if efforts to encourage maximum participation in the wider community are to mean anything. This reasoning makes sense as far as it goes, provided that it does not lead us to forget the inadequacy of the standard PEA for many residents who would be regarded as further towards the "more dependent" end of the continuum.

Regrettably, it has to be said that the message concerning the significance of disposable income and the LA's powers in this respect does not always seem to have got through to SSDs, even as regards "less dependent" residents. For example, I was telephoned by a social worker in the North of England who had arranged for one of his clients, a young man with severe physical disabilities, to move to a hostel in a different LA area, which would be able to cater specifically for his particular care needs and religious requirements. The problem was that the hostel, in line with its rehabilitative philosophy, was insistent that the first LA (which would continue to have financial responsibility) should allow a PEA of at least 40·00 per week. The social worker, who had not been provided with adequate training in this field and who did not have access to the CRAG (which seems to be available to very few - and often only finance - staff in many SSDs) had been solemnly assured by his team leader that the law permitted only the standard PEA. Fortunately for the service user, the social worker in this case had been commendably disinclined to take "no" for an answer and had sought specialist advice. A photocopy of the relevant pages of the CRAG, dispatched from my office, was enough to rescue the placement, but threw into relief the shortcomings in training and information systems, at various levels in the hierarchy, which are too often encountered.

The Treatment of Couples (Residential and Non-residential Care)

In this section, I shall deal with the residential and non-residential settings together, so as to provide a direct comparison between the two, given that as regards benefits and charging, some of the issues are very similar while there are also important differences. (Note that in this discussion I am referring to "couples" and "partners" in the context of heterosexual relationships: homosexual couples of either sex are treated as separate individuals throughout the benefit system as well as in charging arrangements - see "couples" in appendix 3).

Non-means-tested benefits are paid individually to each member of a couple if each has met the various qualifying conditions. Most of these benefits also make provision for additions in respect of partners deemed to be dependent and satisfying various other eligibility criteria. In the case of retirement pension, a dependency addition can be converted into a personal entitlement in certain circumstances. These various rules are complex; require the partners to be married to each other or the dependant to be looking after children for whom the claimant is responsible; and in some cases discriminate against female claimants.

Occupational and private pension schemes have their own rules for the treatment of partners, sometimes subject to state minimum requirements.

Means-tested benefits normally "aggregate" the resources and requirements of couples, regarding the income and capital of each partner as belonging to both. They also extend aggregation to polygamous relationships in the cases of certain ethnic minority cultures. Aggregation will not apply, though, if those concerned cease to be regarded as partners for benefit purposes - for example, if one member of a couple moves permanently into residential care, or both are residents of separate care homes(or clearly living separately even if in the same care home). (See Child Poverty Action Group, 1995a and 1995b for details of means-tested and non-means-tested benefits respectively; these issues are also covered in the section on community care in Disability Alliance, 1995).

The rules for charging for care services, both in the residential and non-residential sectors, require partners to be assessed separately: their income and capital should not be aggregated. There is, in the case of residential or nursing home care, a power then to seek a contribution from the "liable relative" if the partners are married. There is no fixed formula for this, the process being one of negotiation, resolvable in the last resort by a court. SSDs vary in the extent to which they consider it worthwhile to pursue the matter. Certainly, there seems little point where the amount at stake is likely to be small or would cancel itself out by reducing the resident's income support.

Where a charge levied on a resident's income is deemed to have an excessively adverse effect on the position of a partner still at home, the SSD is expected to consider using its discretion to increase the PEA to permit some support to that partner - although the possible effect on the latter's means-tested benefits needs to be considered. (See the CRAG, sections 4,5 and 11 for further details of these various points: DoH and Welsh Office, 1992).

In the case of domiciliary and day care services, there is no power to assess or charge a service user's partner directly. There is scope for the SSD to argue in some cases that the service user can call upon his or her partner's resources, but there is no clear legal framework for this approach, as is reflected in the rather vague and hesitant tone of the DoH note to the Social Services Inspectorate: "Local authorities may, in individual cases, wish to consider whether a client has sufficient reliable access to resources beyond those held in his/her own name for them to be part of his/her means for the purposes of Section 17(3)" (i.e. of HASSASSA). "The most likely instances of this kind will arise in relation to married or unmarried couples. It will be for the authority to consider each case in the light of their own legal advice". (DoH, 1994b, para. 19). In my view, the imprecision of this legislation creates a legal minefield which SSDs would do well to stay out of. Those SSDs which are routinely assessing charges on the basis of both partners' resources are certainly open to legal challenge.

Respite and other Temporary Care

Service users sometimes enter residential care for a temporary period to give a break to a carer. There may also be other reasons for a temporary stay, such as recuperation from an illness or pending adaptation of premises. After eight weeks, normal charging rules apply, including the need to be alert to any continuing domestic expenses. (See "disposable incomes left to residents", above). During the first eight weeks, however, the SSD has the power either to do a full financial assessment, or to charge any other amount which is reasonable. For the avoidance of detailed assessments for short periods, many SSDs avail themselves of this discretion. A number simply charge what is commonly referred to as the "Part 111 minimum": that is, the "basic retirement pension minus PEA" formula. This reflects pre-April 1993 practice, when this was the only alternative course to a full assessment. It discriminates in favour of those who have resources above the basic retirement pension level, as these are ignored; and against those lacking such resources, who are left without any help with home commitments.

Some SSDs have investigated the idea of assuming for the first eight weeks that a temporary resident in the P&V sector receives income at least equivalent to the income support level appropriate to that sector and levying a charge based on that amount. I have no information at the time of writing as to how many SSDs have gone on to adopt this approach, but in my view its rather arbitrary nature leaves it open to legal challenge, certainly where the SSD concerned also places temporary residents with similar care needs in its own homes and charges them less.

It may well be that, in the context of temporary placements in care homes, the fairest way of reconciling administrative facility with revenue-raising objectives and residents' interests would be to seek to devise a simplified version of the full means test. (See chapter 7, though, for a possible alternative to the "charging" approach, for temporary care and otherwise).

Administrative Issues in Residential and Nursing Home Care

A smooth interaction between the benefit system and charging arrangements in respect of residential care and nursing homes represents a considerable administrative challenge. The encouragement of prompt claims (notably for a new award of, or an increase in, income support, as a result of the residential allowance) will be important to the SSD's finances, as will reasonably expeditious processing by the Benefits Agency. The co-ordination of benefit pay days and the levying of charges has to be organised at the beginning of a stay in a care home. Benefits may also fluctuate in the early stages, as AA or DLAC and possibly the income support severe disability premium come and go. Thereafter, other changes of circumstances, such as an increase in occupational pension, have to be notified both to the BA and to the SSD. Respite care presents additional problems, income support changes often lagging behind the pattern of admission and discharge, with HB and council tax benefit to be reckoned with as well. There is no doubt that in the real world, confusion often reigns!

The LA Associations have been attempting to address this set of difficulties partly by negotiating a model service level agreement with the BA. This has not yet come to fruition at the time of writing, although various local versions exist. The objective of the Associations is to secure, with the resident's permission, the automatic exchange of relevant information between LAs and the BA, together with target times for processing. Aside from any other considerations, it is important to residents and those acting on their behalf that these administrative matters should be as "hassle-free" as possible, especially given that there will usually be no reward attaching to the service user's co-operation, the PEA remaining the same whatever happens to the overall benefit level.

Non-residential Services

These include familiar services such as home care, day care and "meals on wheels"; but increasingly sophisticated packages are being developed, sometimes extending to "round-the-clock" coverage, as efforts to support people outside of residential care become more ambitious.

Meanwhile, pressure to charge, or to charge more, for domiciliary and day care services is also increasing. (This process has been documented in research published by the AMA's Anti-Poverty Action unit: AMA, 1994b; and by its successor body, the joint LA Associations' Local Government Anti-Poverty Unit: Harvey and Robertson, 1995). Partly, this is due to the higher cost of more substantial services; but to a great extent, it is a response to the financial pressures described in chapter 3.

Moreover, a deliberate further twist to the upward spiral of charging is provided by the financial machinations of the DoH, which assumes that a certain proportion of SSDs' costs in relation to these services are met through charges and reduces grant support accordingly. As the Department put it in a memorandum to the LA Associations, concerning financial year 1994/5: "What is being *implicitly* assumed is that the rate of recovery is constant across the country - in other words, that the proportion of the gross cost of providing the service which is recovered in charge income is identical in every authority. For simplicity, it would not be far wrong to take this rate to be the current national average recovery rate of about 9 per cent (based on day centres, home care, home helps and meals on wheels). The calculation of the level of central government support for each authority's spending implicitly assumes that some 9 per cent of the gross cost of domiciliary services for the elderly will be recovered in charges". (DoH, 1994c). This obviously puts pressure on those SSDs which recover less than this proportion to increase their charges, which will in turn increase the mean average recovery rate. If the DoH then continues to assume the average, an upward "ratchet" effect will be created, transferring more and more of the costs from central government to the service user.

It should be stressed that this process of increasing charges for community care services contains within it a contradiction. Domiciliary and day care services are supposed to enhance the service user's ability to remain within the community: but charges reduce disposable income and make it harder to afford the basic necessities, such as adequate diet, warm clothing and sufficient heating, which survival in the community demands - quite apart from the need for recreational activities and social contacts. Already, the very high charges levied by some SSDs threaten to create "institutionali-sation in the community", where those concerned receive care services, but can afford to do little else. Conversely, we know that increased charges often cause people to refuse services which they need, because they feel that they cannot afford them.

The legislation contains safeguards - discussed below -which are supposed to afford at least some protection against excessive charges. It is the DoH's contradictory role as custodian of this legislation and as prominent culprit in forcing up charges which leads to that Department's habitually ambiva-lent and evasive tone on the charging question. Meanwhile, SSDs vary in the degree to which they are explicitly conscious of the often self-defeating nature of reducing service users' incomes in order to provide services to help them survive in the community. Many SSDs will argue that they are aware of the problem, but have little choice in the matter.

There are some anecdotal indications that these pressures may be mani-festing themselves in professional attitudes at "grassroots" level also. In one LA where I advised the SSD on the "disposable income" question - and where the ensuing policy still pushed service users below the income support level - several social workers complained to me that not enough revenue was being generated from charges; and bemused finance staff told me that they were now the "new softies", staving off demands from budget-holding social workers to be allowed to charge more.

The growing concern in this field has two broad, if linked, dimensions: the level of charges (contributing to poverty amongst service users); and their lawfulness (the disregard or misunderstanding of service users' rights). I shall look first at the "lawfulness" question.

Lawfulness of Charges for Non-residential Services

Section 17 of HASSASSA governs charging in relation to the services in question and provides, as noted above, certain safeguards. Specifically, "...an authority providing a service...may recover such charge (if any) for it as they consider reasonable" (s17(1)). While if a service user "...satisfies the authority providing the service that his means are insufficient for it to be reasonably practicable for him to pay for the service the amount which he would otherwise be obliged to pay for it, the authority shall not require him to pay more for it than it appears to them that it is reasonably practicable for him to pay" (s17(3)).

There are several points in the above where the precise meaning is not clear. Is the use of a means test enough to satisfy the "reasonably practicable for him to pay" requirement, or must there be a further opportunity to query the charge determined by such a test? Certainly the immovably-fixed flat-rate or hourly charges operated by some SSDs must surely be unlawful.

It also follows from the above that service users have the right to make representations about charges. SSDs which fail to inform them of this are arguably in breach of their duties; while inaccessible information may also be questionable. (See DoH, 1994b, paras. 16-17, which refer to access to information and to relevant Local Government Ombudsman cases concerning the "representations" question. See also, as regards Local Government Ombudsman cases, appendix 1 of AMA and Local Government Information Unit, 1994). The DoH/DoE Framework for Local Community Care Charters in England (DoH and DoE, 1994, para. C6) also refers to the need for information on how to contest decisions on charges - which would sit very uneasily with central government's emphasis on maximising revenue from this source if "affordability" challenges were to take off on a substantial scale. This latter eventuality is far from inconceivable, given rising charges and the apparently growing propensity amongst service users and their representatives to challenge decisions.

Space does not permit an extensive analysis of the full range of legal difficulties which arise from the charging question. For a more detailed treatment, readers should refer to the very useful work produced by the Local Government Information Unit (LGIU) and the AMA (AMA, 1991; AMA and LGIU, 1992; AMA and LGIU, 1994). (These references are also relevant to the "affordability" question discussed below). The following, though, is a brief summary of some of those issues which, in addition to those described above, have particularly attracted comment:

- Services withdrawn if charges are not paid. This is unlawful. The duty to provide appropriate services stands regardless of debts arising from charges, recovery of which can, if necessary, be sought through the courts;

- Services provided (and charged for) at less than the level of need, the service user "topping up" by purchasing "extra" care from the private sector. This constitutes either a failure to assess need adequately (although the questions of what constitutes "need" and of what "meeting need" entails can be vexed); or a failure to fulfil the duty to meet assessed need;

- Routine aggregation of the resources of couples, whereas the law requires them to be considered separately (see "treatment of couples" above);

- Taking into account, for the purposes of charging for non-residential services, the capital value of an owner-occupied home, by placing a charge upon it to be recouped after eventual sale. Some LAs have been considering such an approach. In the non-residential context, this is highly controversial and is likely to face legal challenge if it proceeds.

The DoH advice note for the Social Services Inspectorate addresses most of these legal problems, sometimes helpfully, often evasively. A detailed commentary upon that document (which includes the full text as an appendix) has been published by the AMA and LGIU (1994).

Level of Charges for Non-residential Services

People who live on very low incomes can be placed in serious difficulty even by what might seem to their better-off fellow citizens to be minor reductions in spending power. Charging policies which reduce disposable incomes to amounts near or even below income support levels are therefore to be regarded with concern. As noted above, many LAs may feel that the financial bind into which they have been forced leaves them with little choice if services are to be protected. However, decisions should be taken on the basis of a good understanding of the issues and one factor which regularly muddies these particular waters is a simplistic set of assumptions concerning the role of various social security benefits. Surely, the argument goes, some of these benefits are intended to be used to pay for care? The matter is not, however, that simple. I would like to explore briefly the question of what the key benefits in this context are "for". Their basic features were outlined in chapter 3, but here I would like specifically to consider the question of how far they might be deemed to be available to pay charges for non-residential care services.

The basic rates of *income support* are intended, at least in theory, to cover the costs of food, clothing, fuel and other household necessities. The severe disability premium is considered separately below. The premiums in general replaced payments in the previous (supplementary benefit) scheme which were intended to meet the extra costs of living on benefit for a long period (the "long-term rate") and those which were related to various special needs ("additional requirements"). This last aspect raises the question of whether any element of these premiums could be said to be available for care costs. This is doubtful, as the great bulk of additional requirements payments under supplementary benefit were either for heating or for dietary needs.

Attendance allowance and the *disability living allowance care component,* as noted in chapter 3, have misleading names, in that historically AA (and by extension DLAC, which is closely based upon it) were intended to address the extra costs of severe disability, of which care is only one. Others include extra heating; extra clothing costs due to heavy wear and tear; extra laundry costs; expensive diets; and additional costs caused by limited shopping opportunities. There is also often the cost of help with domestic tasks, which LA domiciliary care services are decreasingly likely to provide. To complicate matters further, the practice is widespread amongst claimants of using at least part of their AA or DLAC to pay for ordinary necessities, reflecting the inadequacy of other benefits for this purpose. It might be argued that if not all, then at least some of a service user's AA or DLAC could be deemed to be available for care costs, but this is at best speculative, given the many other calls on such income.

It should be noted that the social security legislation(section 73(14) of the Social Security Contributions and Benefits Act 1992) precludes the taking into account of the *disability living allowance mobility component* (DLAM) for charging purposes, although I have heard of some apparently unlawful schemes which charge DLAM recipients more than others for mobility-related services such as bus passes or transport to and from day centres.

The income support *severe disability premium* is substantially higher than other premiums and does not "overlap" - that is, it is payable on top of other premiums. It is arguable that it is more reasonable to regard a proportion of this premium as available for charges than is the case with AA or DLAC, but again it should be borne in mind that there are other costs than those relating to care which arise from severe disability. SSDs should also be careful not to assume that the severe disability premium is in payment just because the conditions are met: the BA often fails to spot entitlement.

Can SSDs Square the Circle?

Can the contradictions described in this chapter be resolved by SSDs? I would suggest that compromises between conflicting pressures will frequently be the most that can be achieved, given the existing financial framework. Nevertheless, there is much that can be done to try to limit the difficulties. Not least, SSDs should endeavour to get the law right, or to minimise the grounds for challenge where the law is not clear. They should also take decisions in the light of an adequate understanding of the benefit system. All of this suggests that careful thought will need to be given to the ready availability to all relevant LA councillors and officers of expert advice in the fields of welfare rights and the law relating to charging. This should also feed into training and information systems.

Where contradictory factors are at work, notably revenue- raising versus protection of service users' living standards, it is preferable that these should be highlighted, rather than glossed over, in reports to elected councillors. In this way, informed political, as well as professional, decisions can be made.

Aside from the question of the structure of charging systems, there are also procedural and "quality of service" issues: how charges are administered; what information is provided to service users; how the recovery of arrears is approached and so forth. At the time of writing, the AMA and ACC have recently begun work on the development of guidance in this area.

Increasing attention is being focused upon SSDs' charging policies, especially as regards non-residential care. Research studies are being commissioned or conducted by a number of bodies, including the Social Policy Research Unit at York University, the Disability Alliance and the National Consumer Council; test cases for legal challenges are actively being sought by pressure groups (see chapter 3); around 20 national organisations with an interest in this field have formed a "Coalition on Charging" to campaign on the issues, while local action groups are also springing up (see George, 1995); and the media are taking a growing interest. It may well be that these issues will build up into a source of even greater public and political controversy than is already the case.

Chapter 6

Maximising Claimants' Incomes: The Role of Benefit Checks, Advice and Advocacy

Summary

This chapter considers the importance of benefit take-up to community care service users as well as to SSDs' finances. It argues that there should always be "something in it" for those supported in the community when additional benefit is obtained: the SSD should not see it merely as a source of revenue from charges. The limits of what might be expected of the Benefits Agency in terms of take-up initiatives are considered and conflicts of interest are recognised. The issues around benefit take-up in general and its links with community care in particular are explored. A number of examples of successful take-up work are given. The potential for integrating take-up into community care assessments is considered, including the scope for computerised approaches. Finally, the links are emphasised between ongoing care management and policy in relation to welfare rights advice and advocacy services.

The Importance of Benefit Take-Up

It has been a recurrent theme of this book that disposable income is a very important consideration if vulnerable people are to be able to make their way in the wider community and avoid unnecessary or premature admission into residential care. It therefore follows that people should be helped to ensure that they are receiving all the benefits to which they are entitled.

The above is true not only of service users but also of informal carers. They, too, will often be living on a very low income and their ability to continue caring, as well as their own quality of life, may well be enhanced by due attention to benefit entitlements. Moreover, as Eithne McLaughlin points out (1992,p10), the quality of the relationship between the carer and the person for whom he or she is caring may also be adversely affected by shortage of money. Such relationships between individuals are varied and complex and one should avoid simplistic generalisations, but the capacity of poverty to create or exacerbate stress should never be underestimated. In much of what follows in this chapter, references to efforts to enhance service users' incomes can usefully be considered in the context of benefit take-up amongst carers also. It is, though, preferable for the benefit position of a carer and of the person cared for to be considered in relation to each other, as they can interact: notably, a disabled person cannot receive the severe disability premium if somebody claims the invalid care allowance for looking after him or her. These situations require detailed and sensitive attention.

The potential gains for claimants from "benefit checks" or other initiatives designed to identify unclaimed entitlements can be considerable, as the following examples illustrate:

Illustrations of Benefits which are often Unclaimed

Weekly rates are at 1995/6 values, given before and after a benefit check has been carried out.

Example 1:

Severely disabled young person (aged 30) on severe disablement allowance (SDA) and income support(IS), living alone. Unidentified entitlement to disability living allowance (DLA) (mobility component at top rate; care component at middle rate).

Current income:		
SDA topped up with IS:		£66-30
Income after benefit check:		
SDA + IS (at original level):	£66-30	
DLA:	£63-85	
IS severe disability premium:	£35-05	
	Total:	£165-20
Difference as a result of benefit check:		£98-90

Example 2:

Elderly disabled person (aged 72) on retirement pension and income support, living alone. Unidentified entitlement to lower rate of attendance allowance (AA).

Current income:

Retirement pension (RP) topped up with IS:	£65-10

Income after benefit check:

RP + IS (at original level):	£65-10	
AA:	£31-20	
Higher (instead of ordinary)		
IS pensioner premium = an extra:	£6-55	
IS severe disability premium:	£35-05	
	Total:	£137-90
Difference as a result of benefit check:		£72-80

Example 3:

Elderly disabled person (aged 82) on retirement pension and income support, living alone. Unidentified entitlement to higher rate AA.

Current income:

RP topped up with IS:	£71-65

Income after benefit check:

RP + IS (at original level):	£71-65	
AA:	£46-70	
IS severe disability premium:	£35-05	
	Total:	£153-40
Difference as a result of benefit check:		£81-75

Other examples:

The above gains are very substantial because they relate to people living alone who are entitled to AA (or DLAC at an equivalent rate). Lower but still very worthwhile gains will be more common. For example:

AA and DLAC alone (excluding any extra IS):

highest rate:	£46-70
lower AA/ middle DLAC:	£31-20
lowest DLAC:	£12-40

DLAM:

higher rate:	£32-65
lower rate:	£12-40

HB: can be up to full rent.

Council tax benefit: can be up to full council tax.

These are just examples: the summary of benefits in chapter 3 will suggest others. Miscalculations of benefit (far from infrequent) can also be identified in this way; as can the possibility of payment of arrears.

Benefit take-up is important not only to service users, but also to the finances of SSDs in terms of revenue raised through charges. In the residential sector, every penny of unclaimed benefit on the part of somebody supported financially by the SSD is in this sense a loss to that department. In the non-residential sector, revenue from charges may also be affected. Here, though, it is important that SSDs should not think solely in revenue terms: it should be a cause for concern if, in a given LA, take-up efforts on behalf of those supported in the wider community result only in immediate confiscation of all or most of the proceeds through the charging system. (This returns us to the themes explored in chapter 5).

The examples set out above are couched in terms of a detailed check of entitlements. There are also broader-brush approaches to take-up, which are discussed below. First, though, it might be useful to address the often-asked question: "Surely we should be able to leave all this to the Benefits Agency?"

The Benefits Agency Role

As the body responsible for administering most of the benefits discussed in this book, the BA should indeed be expected to do a good job of it, including the provision of accurate advice to enquirers and good-quality information and publicity. In practice, error rates in adjudication on claims continue to give cause for concern (see e.g. Chief Adjudication Officer, 1994)and - while the BA is committed to improving the standard of advice given by its staff - it is still rash to place too much reliance on being given the right answer when making an enquiry at a local office. In a Consumers' Association survey reported in 1994, advice was sought from 20 offices in different parts of the country, ostensibly by a member of the public on behalf of a 78-year-old woman who was failing to claim a number of important entitlements - income support, AA, HB and council tax benefit. Only 13 offices were able to give the right advice, the rest ranging from the incomplete through the inaccurate to the ludicrous: "The Kilburn office in London gave us a form for sickness benefit, which is for people whose illness prevents them from working". (Consumers' Association, 1994). When confronted with the findings, the BA protested that the survey was too small-scale to be statistically significant (which it did not claim to be) and that the Agency's own consumer surveys showed a high level of satisfaction (Brindle, 1994b). This latter defence represents an important missing of the point: a claimant who has no idea that he or she has been underpaid is hardly likely to express dissatisfaction with the underpayment.

On a similar theme, a representative of the National Association of Citizens' Advice Bureaux (CABx) made the point in 1993 that: "We cannot depend on the Benefits Agency either being aware of changed circumstances or even spotting increased benefit entitlement arising from such changes when they are alerted...CABx are continually reporting cases where carers are not receiving the carer premium with their income support, or people with disabilities are not receiving the disability premiums to which they are entitled". (Rainbow, 1993, p12).

In the broader context of overall levels of take-up, the position is similarly unsatisfactory. Occasionally, a benefit is given an intensive publicity push, but this is invariably tied in with some other political agenda (as in the case of family credit, which is linked to the Government's philosophy on low pay; or poll tax benefit, which was part of the attempt to "sell" the poll tax). Generally, publicity is much lower-key, leaflets rather than television advertising being the order of the day. There is no doubt that there have been improvements: at the time of writing, to take a local example in the area where I work, BA posters inviting requests for information have begun to appear on the Tyneside Metro system, reflecting a more imaginative approach to publicity in at least some parts of the country. More ambitiously, plans are afoot nationally for a "one-stop" approach to claiming a variety of different benefits (although it remains to be seen whether the resources will be forthcoming to make this work). Nevertheless, the Agency still declines to accept responsibility for take-up in terms of percentages of those eligible who actually receive a given benefit: the onus is on the claimant to claim, not on the BA to go out and seek pro-actively to ensure that benefits are taken up. (See Vaux, 1994, for a fuller discussion of this question).

There are, though, limits to what one can expect from the benefit-administering system itself. This is because of conflicts of interest. Although benefits are in theory not cash-limited, in practice budgets exist and pressures which cause spending to exceed expectations are unwelcome. Whenever such "overspending" has occurred, for whatever reason, the Government's usual reaction has been to tighten eligibility criteria and/ or to cut the benefit. It is regrettably rather unworldly to expect an unalloyed crusading zeal for take-up on the part of DSS Ministers, even in the event of a regime more sympathetic to claimants' interests than that currently in place. It might be objected that some LAs have a very good record of encouragement of take-up of the main benefits which they administer - that is, HB and council tax benefit: but this is surely not unrelated to the fact that over nine-tenths of the benefit cost is met by government subsidy. Indeed, higher HB spending (although due mainly to higher rents and greater unemployment rather than to take-up work) has led to repeated government-imposed benefit and subsidy cuts.

At the level of the individual claim, conflicts of interest also operate. While accurate advice and information is surely not too much to ask, the BA cannot be expected to give impartial advice in the event of a disputed decision. This is why the achievement of good-quality administration would not put advice services out of business, as is sometimes fancifully suggested. A proper understanding of conflicts of interest is important to citizens' rights and is, it might be added, the reason why I do not think that advocates dealing with LA benefits and services should be located within the departments which administer them.

Take-up: The Nature of the Problem

It has been well-established at least since the mid-1960s that *means-tested benefits* have a take-up problem. There appear to be several, interacting reasons for this: lack of knowledge amongst potential claimants about complex eligibility criteria(who is eligible, on what sort of income level, how savings are treated and so forth); administrative obstacles (long and complex forms, detailed evidence needed, bad experiences with officials);the stigma associated with means-testing; and a degree of cultural resistance to claiming amongst some ethnic minority communities (see Divine and Vaux, 1988, for a discussion of this last point).

We know that people with more to gain are more likely to claim. This is linked to what other sources of income a person might have to get by on: a pensioner will almost always have a retirement pension of some sort, whereas a single parent may well only have child benefit. Thus, it is not surprising that take-up of income support as a percentage of those eligible is much higher amongst single parents than amongst pensioners. (See DSS, 1994 and 1995, for details of this and other aspects of the take-up estimates referred to below).

The latest government figures (for 1992: see DSS, 1995)suggest that take-up of income support is currently stable; take-up of HB may have fallen slightly compared with the previous year; and take-up of family credit may have improved. Income support is estimated to be reaching somewhere between 77 - 87 per cent of those entitled; HB, somewhere between 88 - 93 per cent; family credit around 73 per cent. (There are no estimates yet for council tax benefit). This, of course, leaves large numbers of people still not claiming their entitlements and offers no grounds for complacency.

The previous year's figures (for 1990-91: see DSS, 1994)suggested that take-up of the main means-tested benefits was creeping upwards compared with earlier years. If we accept this as broadly accurate, we can identify three likely explanatory factors for this apparent improvement, one "positive", one "negative" and one technical, i.e.:

- On the positive side, the cumulative effects of decades of take-up activity, particularly by LAs and perhaps especially, in the last dozen years or so, as regards HB, may now be sufficiently great to be showing up in the overall figures.

- More negatively, as noted above, people with higher means-tested entitlements are more likely to claim (which is why take-up in money terms is always higher than take-up by numbers of claimants); so the erosion of non-means-tested benefits will, other things being equal, push up take-up of means-tested benefits, as will an increase in the proportion of all potential claimants which is constituted by groups with low entitlement to non-means-tested income (relatively more unemployed people and single parents; relatively fewer pensioners). Such an erosion of several important non-means-tested benefits, combined with a shift in the proportions of claimant groups, has indeed occurred in the 1980s and 1990s.

- On a technical point, if take-up has been underestimated to some extent in the past (as the Government suggests) then some of the apparent improvement will be attributable simply to changes in statistical methodology.

It is important to note also that it is not only means-tested benefits which present problems of take-up. We have found since the mid-1970s that *non-means-tested non-contributory disability benefits* such as attendance and mobility allowances (and more recently DLA) also have a take-up problem. This may reflect a resistance to intimate personal questions; and certainly results in part from complex eligibility criteria and daunting application forms. These benefits figure prominently in the examples given below of the under-claiming exposed by various take-up initiatives.

Approaches to Take-up Work

Take-up initiatives are important: they cannot solve the fundamental problems, but they can help large numbers of individuals. They can be traced back to efforts by the unemployed workers' movement in the 1930s and were further developed by the emergent "poverty lobby" in the 1960s and the new LA welfare rights services from the early 1970s. They have been a significant focus of interest for many of those LAs which have developed formal anti-poverty strategies during the 1980s and 1990s (see Fimister, 1994). In such cases, they have often been linked to economic development considerations, recognising that extra central government money drawn into an area via the benefit system will largely be spent within the local economy; and to strategies to enable people on low incomes more readily to afford council tax, council rents and LA charges for services. Within the limitations described above, some useful work has also been done by the BA (and its predecessors).

My own involvement in large-scale take-up exercises began in Newcastle upon Tyne in 1975, with a campaign around housing benefits, followed by campaigns on education benefits, supplementary benefit, disability benefits and so on. As methods have evolved and the benefit system has changed, take-up initiatives have taken different forms over time and in various parts of the country. They have included:

- Advertising in the media;

- Targeting talks or training on particular groups of professionals, other advisers or potential claimants;

- Leaflets, posters and other obvious "paper" methods of communication;

- Intensive work involving benefit checks in specialised contexts, such as day centres and clinics, or amongst low-income groups such as social workers' clients or workers in low-paid occupations;

- Use of administrative records relating to existing awards (taking due note of data protection requirements) to identify other entitlements and invite claims (a method used notably by LAs which have welfare rights and/or anti-poverty strategies and are also HB authorities);

- Exercises undertaken in tandem with new policy or service developments (a good example is the integration of benefit checks into community care assessments, discussed below);

- Exercises undertaken by or with claimants' own self-help organisations. I have noted above that encouragement of benefit claims was one of the concerns of the unemployed workers' movement in the 1930s (see e.g. Supplementary Benefits Commission, 1977, pp 240-1). This tradition has descended, if somewhat sporadically, through organisations such as tenants' associations, claimants' unions and other self-help groups of various sorts. This is highly relevant in the context of community care, where service users' organisations are likely to become increasingly active as the ethos of being prepared to challenge official and professional decisions becomes more firmly rooted. Income is frequently a major concern of service users, so their own organisations will be well-placed to act as a source of information, help and support.

Take-up initiatives which involve members of ethnic minority communities, whether in the community care context or otherwise, require particularly specialised expertise, because of the complex interactions between benefit and immigration law. (Both for information and for an instructive insight into this -one has to say, racist - minefield, see Child Poverty Action Group, 1994). This is an area where individual, detailed advice is far preferable to blanket approaches.

Whatever the type of take-up exercise, organisational considerations are crucial. How much worker or volunteer time will be designated? Which workers or volunteers? How will they be co-ordinated (especially important if more than one agency is involved)? Are all relevant parties involved and informed to the necessary degree? Are available resources adequate to the purpose? In the past, take-up initiatives have run into difficulty by not taking sufficient account of such factors; or by underestimating the need for follow-up advice and advocacy. Although the context will be different, these practicalities apply just as much to initiatives run by community organisations and service user self-help groups as they do to the generally better-resourced exercises mounted by LAs.

It is important to note that take-up campaigns are not a substitute for advice and advocacy services: rather, they generate a demand for such sources of help. A strategy to develop take-up work should therefore run alongside - and be co-ordinated with - a strategy to develop advice and advocacy resources. This in turn needs to be linked to planning and development of community care services. More is said of this below, in the context of ongoing care management.

Take-up Initiatives in the Community Care Context

The LA welfare rights services which grew up in the 1970s were mainly located in SSDs. (A greater diversity of departmental location developed in the 1980s: see Benson, Berthoud and Williams, 1986, for a brief history). Perhaps because of this, it became apparent at an early stage that there was much under-claiming of benefits amongst disabled people and that, as noted above, the problem was not confined to the means-tested variety. In Strathclyde, welfare rights workers found that a highly effective method of seeking out those who were losing much-needed income was to move into an appropriate setting and offer intensive advice and support to the people they met there. Strathclyde Social Work Department was thus able to report a successful onslaught on "a massive shortfall in take-up of benefits" at an occupational and recreational centre for physically disabled people (Casserly and Clark, 1978). Not long afterwards, welfare rights workers in Harlow achieved similar results in a training centre for people with learning disabilities (Bennett and McGavin, 1980).

Variants on this theme began to be developed all over the country. When, in the mid-1980s, I was researching and writing a book on the role of welfare rights work in the personal social services (Fimister, 1986), I had no difficulty in finding a number of highly successful initiatives of this sort: work at a day centre for people with learning disabilities in Coventry (Blunn and Small, 1984); at a day hospital in Birmingham (Davis, 1984); and amongst the clients of community occupational therapists and community health physiotherapists in Islington (Cohen, 1983) - all identified and tackled substantial under-claiming of a range of benefits. Encouragingly, the conduct of the work did not have to be confined to welfare rights experts: with appropriate specialist support, a variety of social work and health staff were able to be involved. (See Davis, 1985, for a discussion of the need for mental health professionals to be aware of and respond to these issues. She includes some excellent illustrative material. Godfrey and Saxton, 1994, convincingly argue a similar case; while Davis, 1994, provides an account of a conference of service users, advocates and mental health workers from the West Midlands which also explored this question).

A decade later, researching and writing this book, it is clear that the problem is undiminished and that exercises along the lines of those described above are needed as much as ever. Recent examples include:

- Work with home care clients in Kirklees and Wandsworth ("More than 2,000 clients could receive an additional 4 million annually in benefits as a result of welfare initiatives in the two authorities": Ivory, 1994b; see also Hayball, 1993);

- Work with home care clients in Sheffield ("Average income for all clients was only 87-13, and the average income gain was 35-46.... In a full year the projected gain for all clients receiving benefits checks in Sheffield is 3.2 million": Alcock and Reid, 1994);

- Work in two health centres in Islington ("A conservative estimate of the total benefit gain by health centre users is 323,000.... a projected average weekly gain for each of the 157 people advised of 39-59": Griffiths, 1992, p4);

- Benefit checks offered at a resource centre for elderly people in Perth ("Claims made resulted in an annual potential increase of some 84,000, or almost 2,000 per client per year, while backdated benefit ranged from a few pounds to several thousands. In many cases benefit was more than doubled...": Crawford and Meechan, 1992, pp 35-6);

- Work by the local CAB in very sheltered accommodation in Kensington ("In total, of the 20 residents seen, 14 increased their incomes by between 31-25 and 72-90 per week": Rainbow, 1993, p12);

- A take-up screening undertaken by mental health social work staff in Solihull ("113 users are now in receipt of DLA totalling 221,863-20 per annum... 48 users have subsequently claimed the severe disability premium on income support totalling 84,115-20 per annum... Relatives and carers of several of the other users have claimed invalid care allowance": Godfrey and Saxton, 1994, p6).

The above are just some of many examples of take-up initiatives which are supporting community care objectives and seeking to compensate for the failure of the benefit system to deliver entitlements to large numbers of very vulnerable people. Many of these are "one-off" exercises, but in some areas they are increasingly becoming an integral part of community care strategies. The incorporation of benefit checks into community care assessments must surely be the way forward.

Integration with Assessments

Several commentators have argued the case for an automatic benefit check for people who are being assessed for community care services (see for example Fimister, 1989; Crawford and Meechan, 1992; Rainbow, 1993). This will secure the advantages described above, for both service user and SSD, of proper attention to take-up; and do so on a systematic basis, rather than leave it to chance involvement of a passing rights initiative or a particularly knowledgeable social worker.

There is the danger that the usually greater financial "stake" which the SSD has in the incomes of people in residential care, as compared with those supported in their own homes, will lead to automatic benefit checks for the former but not for the latter (see Fimister, 1990). For reasons which will be obvious from the discussion in this chapter, this would be a very short-sighted approach. Rather, it is to be hoped that the automatic offer of a benefit check to all service users will soon become the norm.

There are, though, obstacles to be overcome. These are of two kinds: culture on the one hand; and resources combined with pressure of work on the other. As regards culture, there is a long-standing ambivalence within many SSDs concerning the role of welfare rights advice, certainly as regards its place within social work ("Is it our job?") (See Fimister, 1986, chapter 2, for a full discussion). Time will tell whether SSDs' new community care responsibilities will change this. It is noteworthy in this context that recent DoH guidance on continuing care following hospital discharge asserts that: "social services staff should provide written details of the likely cost to the patient of any option which he or she is asked to consider(including where possible and appropriate the availability of social security benefits)". (DoH, 1995, para. 25). It will be interesting to see what, in practice, the words "possible and appropriate" turn out to mean.

Problems with time and resources are more concrete: acquiring new skills and adding further procedures at a time which is already one of pressure and change, often with inadequate or even shrinking resources, can be daunting. As a result, some SSDs which recognise the value of benefit checks have nevertheless yet to introduce them; while others have gone only part of the way. There is much potential as yet unfulfilled.

Use of Computers

Strongly to be recommended is the use of computer technology in developing a system of benefit checks. There are now a number of software packages on the market which are both highly accurate and relatively easy to learn to use. Nor do they need to be expensive. They can take the person inputting the information concerning the service user's circumstances step-by-step through the benefits labyrinth, checking the accuracy of existing awards and identifying unclaimed entitlements. "What if?" calculations are also possible, indicating the different benefit outcomes of varying sets of circumstances.

Attention needs to be paid to back-up support such as training in the use of the system, preferably complemented by basic benefit training; advice in case of problems, both on the benefit and on the computer aspects; and efficient distribution of software updates. Interviews with service users and/ or those acting on their behalf are generally not likely to take place in the social services office, so data-gathering methods such as forms or checklists will need to be considered where portable computers are not available. SSDs which have access to a specialist welfare rights service will be better placed than others to achieve a comprehensive set of arrangements; but others will find most software suppliers ready to be helpful in overcoming difficulties. In Newcastle, using the Lisson Grove package, the Welfare Rights Service provides the back-up support in association with the SSD's computer specialists and - while we have yet to achieve our objective of fully integrating benefit checks into the community care assessment process - we have developed a network of system users (drawing from a variety of professional callings and including some city councillors) on over 40 different sites. (For a fuller discussion of Newcastle's experience, see Fimister, 1993c).

As this is a field which changes rapidly, I shall not seek to discuss the pros and cons of different software packages. Suffice it to say that readers interested in exploring this approach are advised to try out several, testing them with the help of potential system users and preferably with advisers knowledgeable about benefits. Accuracy should not normally be a problem, but some packages may be more suited to your particular needs than others.

Role of Welfare Rights Specialists

It will be apparent from the above that I do not consider it necessary - or even sensible, given scarce resources - for routine benefit checks to be assigned to welfare rights specialists. The latter would be more appropriately deployed as a resource, providing input to policy planning, training and other back-up. Their direct involvement in individual cases will be best reserved for those which become problematic for one reason or another. (See the discussion of ongoing care management below; and see Fimister, 1986, chapter 3, for a fuller discussion of a "welfare rights resource").

From the viewpoint of welfare rights specialists, the new community care arrangements present many opportunities, but also some problems. There is the obvious danger of acquiring new duties without additional resources. There are also potential ethical difficulties, as a welfare rights advocate has a duty towards claimants: he or she is not just a "benefits technician". This can create difficulties, particularly when advice is sought by SSDs from the welfare rights adviser on technical aspects of charging policies. The role of the adviser should be to get the best possible deal for the claimant, but this might not always be clearly recognised. Practical and ethical issues relating to the role of welfare rights workers in the community care context are explored in a document produced by the National Welfare Rights Officers' Group (now the National Association of Welfare Rights Advisers)(National WROG, 1991).

Advice, Advocacy and Care Management

It remains to make the point that it is not enough merely to provide a service user with a "snapshot" of his or her current benefit entitlement. Help may be needed with claims. Moreover, circumstances change and new problems arise. The concept of continuing care management, if it is to be credible, requires that service users should be put in touch with appropriate sources of advice and advocacy when needed and that outcomes should be monitored.

People cannot, of course, be put in touch with services which are not actually available, which means that community care policy needs to be considered alongside policies in relation to the provision of advice services (whether the LA provides them directly or by supporting the voluntary sector or both). This will be a challenge to those SSDs which have traditionally seen this area as peripheral to their interests; and will require corporate thinking and working where the SSD is not the lead department for advice service provision.

Advice services have many roles and should not merely be dissolved into community care arrangements, but a care management strategy which ignores the advice dimension will be failing the service user.

Chapter 7

Community Care and the Benefits System: Should we Start Again?

"Well, you can do it without me!" (Horrified senior social services manager upon hearing the title of this chapter).

There is a serious point to the above quotation. We should not underestimate the potential disruption to services and to the lives of service users and informal carers which is inherent in any large-scale changes. Such changes should not be undertaken without strong justification.

Nevertheless, it is apparent from the issues set out in this book that the benefit system is causing problems within the community care context. Complexity, inadequacy, policy contradictions, apparently unintended consequences as well as deliberate cutbacks, abound. As noted in chapter 1, consultations are ongoing between the LA Associations and the DoH, DSS and BA: but these are concerned with details rather than fundamentals; proposals which might have even quite modest resource implications are unlikely to progress very far.

In this concluding chapter, I would like to highlight some points which I believe require further discussion - professional, political and public - over the next few years. I shall not claim or attempt, in the space available, to do full justice to the important issues which they raise. Some of them, indeed, would require a book to themselves. Rather, they are put forward as headings for debate which arise logically from the conclusions drawn in the foregoing chapters.

It will be readily apparent that a number of the suggestions made in this chapter have, to one degree or another, significant cost implications. This raises the question of political realism.

The Political Dimension

If one raises the question of additional spending, especially in respect of one of the more expensive possibilities for change such as a service free at the point of delivery (discussed below), one is apt to be told that "the taxpayer cannot afford it". We should not, however, allow the debate to be stifled by this ploy, for this is not a statement of fact, but rather of a political agenda. If all of our citizens are to have access to decent services, then they have to be paid for. If it is said that the taxpayer cannot afford them but somebody else can - for example, the service user through charges or private insurance - then this is either insincerely meant (that is, it is a deceitful camouflage of the view that many of our poorer citizens will not be able to have decent services); or it is a political statement about where the burden of cost should fall. Income tax; national insurance contributions; inheritance taxes; corporate taxes; indirect taxes; charges to service users.... All are different ways of raising money which have different distributional impacts on different sections of society. These are matters for political decision, not immutable Acts of God.

Clearly, the Government in place at the time of writing cannot realistically be expected to undertake a redistribution of costs and resources which would favour the less, at the expense of the more, affluent. This would be a reversal of the distributional tendency of its economic, fiscal and social policies since 1979. Moreover, the Government has a view of the international economy and its requirements which does not bode well for the share of national resources which might in future be bent towards social purposes (see for example Lilley, 1993). We should therefore be aware of the limited scope for argument here- although of course new lobbying possibilities have opened up as a result of the Government's dwindling Parliamentary majority.

As regards the official Opposition, although the overall tone emphasises greater fairness, it is also one of electoral caution: the more affluent vote is courted assiduously, with the danger that public spending plans, when the details emerge, maybe rather unambitious because of a reluctance to disturb the existing distribution of resources except perhaps at the very top. The Commission on Social Justice, set up by the former Labour leader, the late John Smith, was technically independent of the Labour Party, but certainly went about its business with one eye on what was likely to fit in with the Opposition's approach. The consequent report - with its mixture of good intentions, good and not so good ideas, caution and imprecision - reflects this. (Commission on Social Justice, 1994. See Fimister, 1995, for a commentary on the social security and personal taxation aspects).

It therefore seems that those who wish to see a much better deal for people on low incomes - community care service users or otherwise - are going to continue to face something of an uphill struggle for some time to come. While the outcome of the next general election will certainly have a crucial effect on the gradient of the hill - and on whether we may be able to push up it or continue to slide down - it will remain essential to do our best to articulate and de-mystify the political choices to be made in the field of social policy, if the needs of the less advantaged are to be given proper consideration.

This returns us to the specific policy questions which are raised by the subject of this book. They are couched in terms of a short list of issues which a Government well-disposed towards the interests of service users might want to re-think. I do not suggest that they are comprehensive - one could derive many more from the foregoing chapters - but they are, I think, amongst the most important.

"Free at the Point of Delivery"?

The National Health Service is still largely free at the point of delivery (although as noted in chapters 3 and 4, patients' benefits are reduced at various stages of a stay in hospital). Should not the principle of a free service apply also to community care services - both residential and non-residential? This would place upon the tax system the burden which currently falls upon service users via the charging process. Given the potential for hardship and injustice which surrounds the charging approach (see chapter 5) this idea has much to commend it.

Attractive though this proposal may be, it does raise a number of questions (apart from the political one of distribution of costs) which would require careful consideration. Firstly, should SSDs retain the lead organising role? That is, should we perhaps, after all, do it without the dismayed social services manager quoted at the beginning of this chapter? There would certainly be an argument to be made that a service closely related to health care which was free at the point of delivery would be more appropriately located with the NHS. On the other hand, such major disruption of the assessment and care management arrangements which have developed in the last few years would be hard to justify and there is, indeed, no reason why it would be impossible for SSDs to continue with their lead role, working alongside the NHS, under this proposal.

In this case, though, the financial arrangements with central government would need a lot of work. LAs should be careful here. As Michael Hill and I have argued in relation to both community care and HB: "...the delegation of such powers to local government, in the context of tight resource controls, creates a situation in which local implementers of central policies seem to have to take the blame for some of the individual consequences of those policies. This we contend is a central issue for central-local relations in the 1990s". (Fimister and Hill, 1993, p112. This is pertinent also to the wider question of "localisation", discussed below).

A formula for "downrating" of benefits for care home residents would presumably replace the charging system. This should be looked at alongside a review of the corresponding formula for hospital patients (see chapter 3), which is often punitive and badly needs an overhaul.

The difficult boundaries between hospitals, care homes and the various types of "housing with care" arrangement (certain hostels, group homes, supported lodgings and so forth) need to be reviewed (see below). A new dimension would be added to this, though, if social as well as health care services were free at the point of delivery. There would be questions to be addressed as to which types of accommodation should be entirely free of charge and which should entail a rental element. This would in turn have implications for the income support residential allowance and possibly for the HB scheme.

Prescriptions, dental and optical treatment should be included in those services which are free at the point of delivery. The present complex means tests, as a result both of low take-up and of limited eligibility, exclude large numbers of people who cannot afford to pay charges.

A Social Insurance Approach?

An alternative approach, which might have the virtue of better protecting the financial position of LAs, would be to continue with charges, but enable service users to meet them through the national insurance scheme. Such a system is in the process of implementation in Germany (European Commission, 1994)and the idea has been smiled upon by the Commission on

Social Justice (1994, p301). I do not have space to discuss the detailed issues which arise from this. Suffice it to say that the adequacy and fairness of any given scheme should be judged against two key criteria:

- Do the benefits meet the cost of assessed care needs? We do not want to re-create the "shortfall" problem (see chapters 2 and 3) in another form; and

- Who, if anybody, is excluded? As noted in chapter 3, national insurance contributions are in fact an earmarked tax rather than payments into a true insurance scheme. This creates the potential for an inclusive approach which does not discriminate against those who have been disadvantaged in terms of previous labour market participation. A scheme which is financed on a contributory basis can nevertheless provide access without operating contribution tests to exclude those who, for reasons such as unemployment, disability or caring responsibilities, have not been able to build up contribution records. (See Fimister and Lister, 1981). Conventionally, though, contribution tests of one sort or another are applied to national insurance benefits. A good way of identifying weaknesses in a given scheme is therefore to ask hard questions about who is left out. Note that a system which did not entail contribution-tested barriers to entitlement could be linked to a comprehensive disability income scheme (see below).

The question of the financing of community care, especially the long-term care needs of elderly people, is destined to become increasingly the subject of public debate (see Laing, 1993, for a discussion of options). The Commission on Social Justice has called for "...a far fuller enquiry than we have been able to carry out ourselves, to develop funding options and seek agreement on the best way forward" (1994, p301). Whichever approach emerges in due course, it is certain to be tied up with the social security system to one degree or another.

What other issues might be on the agenda of a government which is serious about tackling the problems around social security and community care?

Benefit Regimes in Different types of Accommodation

I shall not say a great deal about this question in this final chapter, as the chaos here was described in detail in chapter 4. I should emphasise, though, that a review of the position is required, with a remit to sort the difficulties out rather than to seek further benefit savings. In particular, an alternative to the "registration test" must be found; and access to AA and DLAC clarified and protected.

Disability Benefits

The cutbacks in entitlement caused by the replacement of invalidity benefit with incapacity benefit should be reviewed and revised to create a fair and adequate payment to compensate for reduced or absent earning capacity. This benefit should be neither means-tested nor contribution-tested and should also replace the severe disablement allowance, which is plainly inadequate.

Linking with the previous heading in this chapter, the availability of AA and DLAC should be reviewed. At present, many people in community-based supported accommodation are refused benefit on the spurious grounds that the LA should or might be able to support them.

Ideally, the addressing of these specific problems in relation to disability benefits should be part of a wider reappraisal designed to achieve a more adequate and more coherent overall system. Disability benefits have developed into a complex jumble of measures which generally fail to meet need and which vary radically depending on factors including the cause of disability and the employment record of the disabled person. These variations are partly historical and partly represent notions of "deservingness". What is needed is an overhaul which would lead to the phasing in of a comprehensive system designed to provide an earnings replacement benefit for those with partial or total incapacity for work; plus an allowance paid regardless of working capacity, based on the severity of disability and designed to meet the consequent extra costs of living.

A wide range of organisations concerned with disability have backed the idea of such a "comprehensive disability income scheme". The objectives are concisely summarised by the Disability Alliance: "Equity between people with disabilities and non-disabled people - through measures to raise the living standards of people with disabilities to those of non-disabled people. Equity among people with disabilities - so that people with different types of condition - whether physical, mental or sensory, whether from birth or acquired in the home, at work or at war - have a right to income on equal terms. Equity between degrees of disability - by assessing the severity of disability, so that amounts of benefit vary according to the degree and not the type of disability. A Comprehensive Disability Income would be available to all people with disabilities as of right; regardless of age, sex, race, marital status or national insurance record". (Hadjipateras and Witcher, 1991).

Carers

It should be remembered that, often - as noted in chapter 1 - the earning potential of informal carers is, or has in their past been, severely curtailed. Many carers are themselves elderly and vulnerable and many are poor. The invalid care allowance is inadequate both in amount and in scope, but could provide the basis of a more realistic means of support for those who have sacrificed earnings for caring responsibilities. Its amount would need to be increased and its availability greatly extended (see below).

The question of support for carers has become a subject of increasing debate. One recent development which was perhaps unexpected was the Government's decision to support Labour MP Malcolm Wicks's (1995) private member's bill, the Carers' Recognition and Services Bill, giving carers the right to their own community care assessments. LAs will be required to "take into account" the results of such assessments, a duty which falls short of a firm requirement to provide services. Nevertheless, public expectations will have resource implications which promise to be the focus of new controversy.

Carers' assessments will sometimes entail a problem not only of resources but also of reconciling the wishes of the carer and of the person cared for, which may not coincide. If, as a matter of good practice, both parties' assessments include a benefit check, a similar difficulty may be encountered within the social security system. As noted in chapter 6, an award of invalid care allowance to the carer will disentitle the disabled person to the severe disability premium (which forms part of the income support calculation and can also be relevant to HB and council tax benefit). This "trap" needs to be removed so as to end a troublesome conflict of interest:

the benefits of the person cared for should not be adversely affected by those which the carer receives. The extra costs of severe disability are considerable and it should not be assumed that this premium has to be spent on remunerating the carer. The latter should been titled to a benefit in his or her own right to replace earnings which the caring role so often precludes or diminishes.

If the invalid care allowance is to play a more substantial role, then not only must the level of payment be improved, but entitlement must cease to depend on receipt by the disabled person of benefits which are paid only for the more severe degrees of disability. (Similar points have been made by the House of Commons Social Services Committee: 1990b, paras. 106-7).Before governments dismiss such arguments as expensive wishful thinking, they should pause to consider the cost of not making the caring role more financially secure. Especially as female participation in the paid labour force increasingly consolidates itself, the supply of unpaid carers may not be so readily available in the future. As Laing puts it, the "...massive contribution of unpaid care dwarfs the amount of paid long-term care services..." and if carers withdrew from this role on any significant scale, there would be "...catastrophic effects... on local authority care budgets". (Laing, 1993, p14). It should be noted in this context that the British Medical Association (BMA)has recently estimated that the care provided by informal carers is saving the Government at least 33 billion per year. (BMA, 1995).

Lump-sum Grants for Essential Needs

A system of entitlements to "start-up" grants for people being resettled into the community from hospital or residential care should replace the arbitrary and cash-limited "community care grants" (sometimes) provided by the Social Fund. This should be seen as part of a wider need to re-establish a system of grants in place of the Social Fund which, as noted in chapter 3, is based on the hazardous and irresponsible policy of offering loans to people already on extremely low incomes.

Several sets of proposals have been put forward for replacing the Social Fund - for example, by Craig (1990); Berthoud (1991); and the Social Security Advisory Committee (SSAC) (1992). These proposed schemes have a lot of similarities, although Craig's is the most robust in terms of largely ruling out loans. The SSAC version has been specifically endorsed by the Commission on Social Justice, which describes the Social Fund as

"Perhaps the most soul-destroying aspect of Income Support..." (1994, p252). This approach entails replacing the Fund with a three-tier structure: periodic payments to help with predictable larger costs; payments for specified crises, such as a cooker breaking down; and a residual discretionary power to meet special needs. It is not clear from the Commission on Social Justice report what role if any would still be played by loans under its proposals, although their ill-effects are roundly condemned. One could discuss the detail of this sort of structure at length, but it is sound in principle, subject to the elimination of loans (except for emergency payments to non-benefit claimants on higher incomes).

"Localisation"

I have discussed above a number of changes which could usefully be made in current patterns of service and benefit provision. I would like now to consider a change of direction which is increasingly finding its way onto the Government's agenda and which, far from being welcome, poses considerable hazards for service users, benefit claimants and LAs. I refer to "localisation", which - in the sense in which the term is used in the current debate - does not mean the devolution of administration to local or neighbourhood level, but rather the shifting of problematic responsibilities from central to local government.

I remarked in chapter 2 that, although the thrust of central government policy towards local government has in recent times been very much concerned with eroding the powers of the latter, two notable exceptions were the new HB scheme of 1982/3 and the post-Griffiths community care responsibilities implemented from April 1993. In both cases, the legal and financial frameworks were designed to preserve as far as possible central government's effective control over the key elements, while difficult operational matters were "exported" to local government along with the attendant vulnerability to public criticism for controversial outcomes, including those arising from under-financing. (See Fimister and Hill, 1993).

There is much ambivalence amongst LA interests when offered additional powers along these lines. The "poisoned chalice" aspect is increasingly well-understood, but any relief from the general trend of declining powers is inevitably seductive.

There are now strong signs, certainly in the social security context, that the potential of such "localisation" for controlling costs, while also exporting operational problems and blame, is becoming increasingly attractive to central government. This is an outcome of the ongoing search for savings, presided over by the Secretary of State under pressure from the Treasury.

In a speech to the Social Market Foundation on 9th. January 1995, Peter Lilley, the current Secretary of State for Social Security, ranged over several of the main cutbacks to benefit entitlements either planned or recently implemented, including the replacement of sickness and invalidity benefits with incapacity benefit, the replacement of unemployment benefit with the jobseeker's allowance and cuts to HB and to income support payments for mortgage interest. He added ominously that it would be "dangerously complacent to halt the process of reform" and went on to ask "...whether all social security benefits should be uniform nationally and centrally administered". A national system "...has many advantages - economies of scale, avoiding disparities and inequities, and preventing internal benefit tourism. But it means local provision cannot be tailored to local circumstances. It becomes harder to bring local knowledge to bear on the delivery of benefit. It is harder to mobilise local pride to generate positive alternatives to welfare dependency... I do not conclude that the whole benefit system should be localised. But whenever changes are made in future I will consider cautiously whether some greater degree of localisation could bring improvements". (Lilley, 1995, pp 4-5).

As the BA already operates mainly via a system of local districts, it is clear that Lilley is not referring merely to the geographical location of buildings. Given the cautionary tales provided by the examples of HB and community care responsibilities (both of which Lilley cites in support of his case) the prospect of further "localisation" by the present Government must be viewed with concern. Geographical inconsistency of treatment of claimants/ service users; unacceptable variation in standards; eccentric distribution of resources in an overall context of under-financing - these are the classic objections to a locally-fragmented benefit system and they are all associated with HB and community care services.

I would like to go on to look briefly at two areas where "localisation" is currently a very topical issue: the latest round of HB cuts, scheduled for October 1995 (although, as noted in chapter 3, it is possible that this timetable could slip); and the proposal to provide SSDs with powers to make direct payments to disabled people for the purchase of care services.

1. The proposed October 1995 cuts to HB.

I described briefly in chapters 3 and 4 the Government's plans to restrict HB for new claimants in the private deregulated sector (and in respect of some housing association tenants). For those who cannot move or persuade their landlord/ landlady to reduce the rent, this could entail very severe hardship. The existing protection which requires the payment of full benefit to members of certain "vulnerable groups" (elderly or disabled people and families with children) unless suitable alternative accommodation is available and it would be reasonable for them to move, will be abolished, along with the DSS subsidy on the "high rent" element.

Clearly, there is the potential here for considerable scandal and some high-profile "horror stories" if elderly and disabled people and children are to be subject to the full rigours of such a regime. The Government therefore proposes to distribute to HB authorities a small discretionary fund, to be used to bail out cases of "exceptional hardship". Indications at the time of writing are that the Government will make available about one-third of the amount which would be needed to protect all claimants who are "vulnerable" on the existing definition. HB authorities would be permitted to spend a similar amount from their own funds, leaving the other third without protection. Central government will thus make savings while potentially hostile media enquiries in any given case can be referred to the HB authority's "localised" discretionary powers.

It should be added that, not only are there knock-on implications here for LAs' homelessness responsibilities under housing legislation, but SSDs' powers and duties under community care legislation and the Children Act 1989 are also likely to come under pressure. At the time of writing, the LA Associations are pressing the DSS to make clear how it sees these various sets of responsibilities interacting. It may well suit the Department to allow the mess to be "resolved locally".

2. Direct payments to disabled people.

In constructing packages of care services, SSDs do not at the time of writing have powers to make payments direct to the service user so that the latter can pay for his or her own preferred care arrangements. Many disabled people would prefer to be able to exercise this degree of personal control and many SSDs do in fact get round their lack of powers by using "laundering" arrangements via trusts or other "third parties". (See Nadash and Zarb, 1994). Widespread support for the extension to SSDs of the power to make direct payments is to be found amongst organisations representing disabled people, the LA Associations and professional bodies within the Social Services world. The DoH, initially unenthusiastic, is now also a convert and the Secretary of State for Health has declared her intention to progress the matter. Preliminary discussions between the DoH and the LA Associations have commenced.

In my view, the case is very strong for service users to have the right to support in the form of direct payments for care services. Obviously, the question of the adequacy of such payments would need to be addressed. Moreover, given that direct payments would in many cases be used to employ carers, work also needs to be done on finding a means of guaranteeing adequate remuneration and other terms and conditions of employment (an aspect of this debate to which sufficient weight has not so far been given). Whatever further work is required, though, there are no insuperable obstacles in the way of such a development.

Nevertheless, I would question the uncritical assumption that a system of direct payments has necessarily to be run by the local authority SSD. There are considerable difficulties and potential hazards in this approach which have been too readily brushed aside in the general enthusiasm for the overall principle of direct payments.

Firstly, SSDs have had, since the early 1960s, cash-giving powers under children's legislation, which have reacted uneasily with parallel social security provision, causing persistent "boundary disputes" as to which agency has responsibility to meet which type of need in which kind of situation. (See, amongst many discussions of this issue, Hill and Laing, 1978; Fimister, 1980).This long-standing controversy was, moreover, given a new boost in the context of the Children Act 1989, which enhanced LAs' powers in this area; and of the community care debate, when the Griffiths Report proposed that the community care grant element of the Social Fund budget should be transferred to SSDs. (Griffiths, 1988, para. 6.8. See Davies, 1988, for an astute critique of the idea).

These experiences have, on the whole, confirmed the attitude in LA circles in the UK that benefit-type functions on the part of SSDs should be kept to a minimum. Tied in with this are ideas that the social security (including the social assistance) system needs to be national to ensure consistent adjudication and resourcing (see above); and that the move away from local Poor Law-derived approaches to social assistance is at least one aspect of UK benefit policy where we have got it right in comparison with some continental alternatives. The "gatekeeping" role in relation to community care funds has further blurred this divide (Becker, 1996, will include a discussion of this point); but this does not so far involve benefit-style direct cash payments.

Secondly, it might be very hard to guarantee the adequacy of direct payments within the context of the local government finance machinery. We need only look as far as the serious resource shortages which are causing so much trouble in the mainstream of community care finance to find reason to be surprised at the ready trust which seems to be afforded to central government in the matter of grant support for direct payments.

A move by SSDs to a direct cash-providing role in the context of disability would also carry with it a threat to the future of benefits such as AA, DLAC and the disability-related premiums within the means-tested schemes. It is easy to envisage Ministers at some future date pleading "duplication", invoking "localisation" and setting up a new "transfer of funds" to dissolve these benefits into the local government finance system, with all the attendant problems of inadequacy, distributional eccentricity and loss of rights.

An alternative and in my view altogether more desirable approach would be to build a "direct payment for care" element into the national social security system, preferably as part of the comprehensive disability income scheme referred to above. (This would be consistent also with a non-contribution-tested social insurance approach to care funding - again, see above).Service users would need to "opt into" this, so as to enable those who wished instead to receive a package of services arranged by the SSD to do so. "Opting in" would help to ensure also that SSDs could not simply channel service users in this direction so as to relieve pressure on their own funds. Much work would need to be done on procedures for the assessment of care needs (since a single standard rate of payment would be far too much of a blunt instrument). This could lie with the SSD on a sub-contracted basis or with a separate service linked to the BA. There would also be estimates and adjustments to be made concerning the relative overall effects on LA and BA spending.

Such an approach would swim against the stream of the DSS's desire to extricate itself from care costs (see chapter 2); but would help to avoid some worrying pitfalls. The "direct payments" debate did not emerge from the "localisation" agenda and I do not suggest that the DoH's change of heart on the matter was significantly (if at all) influenced by developments across the river at the DSS. Nevertheless, the two sets of issues have coincided in a potentially damaging way, which a strong link to the national social security system could counteract.

In summary on the question of "localisation": our hypothetical benign government should examine its current extent; halt its progress; seek to repair the damage inflicted by measures such as the October 1995 HB cuts; and establish a consultative process to consider what alternative structures might be desirable in the long term as regards the rights of disabled people in respect of payments for care.

Benefit Checks, Advice and Advocacy

There remains one final item on the "shopping list" of issues set out in this chapter. If rights to income are to mean anything to the large numbers of service users and carers who are unaware of their entitlements or have problems in claiming them, then a review must be undertaken of the availability of benefit checks, advice and advocacy within the community care context(see chapter 6). Such a review should involve representatives not only of central and local government, service users and carers, but also of the various advice networks in the non-governmental sector. The relationship of benefits advice to other forms of advice should form part of these deliberations, with a view to ensuring access to comprehensive support.

Information, advice and advocacy and their availability to community care service users is but one aspect of the much wider question of access to such resources on the part of the population as a whole. This is too large an issue to begin to address here, but it is now nearly twenty years since the National Consumer Council (NCC) declared such access to be a "right of citizenship" (NCC, 1977) and we are still a very long way from achieving this.

A Political Lead

At a number of points in this chapter I have referred to the need for a review of this or that provision. This has to be approached with caution. At present, the work of central government departments in the community care field often reflects narrow departmental agendas which do not necessarily mesh with each other or fit well with service users' and carers' best interests. A government committed to constructive change would need to address this, tackling policy conflicts and ensuring that departments were pulling together. This may well prove something of an acid test of this hypothetical regime's sincerity, since - as I have argued elsewhere (Fimister, 1988, p35) - it can be convenient to government to allow policy conflicts to persist, if attempts to resolve them would have resource implications which could expose overall priorities to criticism.

Thus, bravely, the policy review or reviews which would be needed to re-think the areas discussed should:

- involve all relevant government departments and agencies, as well as local government and appropriate non-governmental organisations including those representative of service users and carers;

- be given a clear political remit to address the given problems, not find traditional departmental rationales for dodging them.

Resources would, of course, be needed to make a reality of the proposals for changes to benefits and services which would emerge from such scrutiny. This would require changed priorities in relation to taxation and public spending.

As I said at the beginning of this chapter, the issues set out above require public, professional and political discussion over the remaining few years of the 1990s. We should ask ourselves honestly, as members of a relatively affluent - albeit unequal - society, whether we have a community care system which is good enough to bequeath to the 21st. Century.

References

Age Concern (1989)
Moving the Goalposts: Changing Policies for Long-Stay Health and Social Care of Elderly People, briefing paper, London: Age Concern England.

Alcock, P. and Reid, P (1994)
Taking Charge, Community Care, 30.4.94

Association of County Councils (1994)
Community Care Funding Arrangements: Community Care Funding in 1994/95 and 1995/96, memorandum to Dept. of Health, Dec., London: ACC.

Association of County Councils and Association of Metropolitan Authorities (1994)
Unpublished working paper, London: ACC/ AMA.

Association of County Councils, Association of Directors of Social Services and Association of Metropolitan Authorities (1994)
Guidance on Contracting for Residential and Nursing Home Care for Adults, London: ACC/ ADSS/ AMA.

Association of Metropolitan Authorities (1993)
Community Care and the Registration of "Small Homes" from April 1993: Effects on Benefits and Charging, Social Services Circular 37/93, 17.5.93, London: AMA.

Association of Metropolitan Authorities (1994a)
Community Care Funding and the 85 Per Cent STG Rule, paper to Local Government Finance Settlement Working Group, SWG(94)14, London: AMA.

Association of Metropolitan Authorities (1994b)
A Survey of Social Services Charging Policies 1992-1994, London: AMA.

Association of Metropolitan Authorities and Local Government Information Unit (1991)

Too High a Price?: Examining the Cost of Charging Policies in Local Government, London: AMA/ LGIU.

Association of Metropolitan Authorities and Local Government Information Unit (1992)

A Review of Issues Relating to Charging for Community Care Services, Dec., London: AMA/ LGIU.

Association of Metropolitan Authorities and Local Government Information Unit (1994)

Commentary on Social Services Inspectorate Advice Note on Discretionary Charges for Adult Social Services, London: AMA/ LGIU.

Audit Commission (1986)

Making a Reality of Community Care, London: HMSO.

Audit Commission (1994)

Taking Stock: Progress with Community Care, London: HMSO.

Baldwin, S. (1988)

Introduction to Baldwin, S.; Parker, G.; Walker, R. (eds.), Social Security and Community Care, Aldershot: Avebury.

Balloch,S. and Robertson, G. (eds.) (1995)

Charging for Social Care, London: Local Government Anti-Poverty Unit/ National Institute for Social Work.

Becker, S. (1996)

Responding to Poverty: Cash, Care and Control, London: Longman (forthcoming).

Becker, S., Walsh, M. and Warden, A. (1990)

Sentenced to Live Within That Sickness: Mental Health, Social Security and Registered Homes, Nottingham: Nottinghamshire County Council Welfare Rights Service/University of Nottingham Benefits Research Unit.

Bennett, T. and Mc.Gavin, P. (1980)

Benefiting from Good Advice, Community Care, 31.7.80.

Benson, S., Berthoud, R. and Williams, S. (1986)

Standing Up for Claimants: Welfare Rights Work in Local Authorities, London: Policy Studies Institute.

Berthoud, R. (1991)

Unpicking the Social Fund, Poverty, no. 79, Summer.

Berthoud, R. and Casey, B. (1988a)

The Cost of Care in Hostels, London: Policy Studies Institute.

Berthoud, R. and Casey, B. (1988b)

Do They Really Care?, Community Care, 15.9.88.

Betteridge, J. and Davis, A. (1990)

Cracking Up: Social Security Benefits and Mental Health Users' Experiences, Manchester Welfare Rights Service/ Mental Health and Welfare Rights Network/ University of Birmingham (Dept. of Social Policy and Social Work), London: MIND Publications.

Blunn, C. and Small, M. (1984)

The Anomalies of Attendance Allowance, Community Care, 16.2.84.

Bradshaw, J. (1988)

Financing Private Care for the Elderly, in Baldwin, S.; Parker, G.; Walker, R. (eds.), Social Security and Community Care, Aldershot: Avebury.

Bradshaw, J. and Hood, C. (1977)

Dilemma of a Quango, New Society, 13.1.77.

Brindle, D. (1994a)

Care Ruling "Could Cost NHS Dear", news item, Guardian, 3.2.94.

Brindle, D. (1994b)

Survey of 20 Benefits Offices "Too Small to be Reliable": "Poor Advice" Claims Dismissed by Agency, news item, Guardian, 7.4.94.

Brindle, D. (1994c)

NHS Care for Old to be Limited, news item, Guardian, 8.7.94.

British Medical Association (1995)

Who Cares for the Carers?, London: BMA.

Burgess, P. (1994)

Opening a Can of Worms, Community Care, 3.3.94.

Casserly, J. and Clark, B. (1978) — A Welfare Rights Approach to the Chronically Sick and Disabled, Glasgow: Strathclyde Regional Council.

Chief Adjudication Officer (1994) — Annual Report of the Chief Adjudication Officer 1993-1994, London: HMSO.

Child Poverty Action Group (1994) — Ethnic Minorities' Benefits Handbook (to be periodically revised), London: CPAG.

Child Poverty Action Group (1995a) — National Welfare Benefits Handbook (annually revised), London: CPAG.

Child Poverty Action Group (1995b) — Rights Guide to Non-Means-Tested Benefits (annually revised), London: CPAG.

Clark, S. (1994) — Funding Rules Force Elderly to Leave Home, news item, Community Care, 14.4.94.

Clements, L. (1994) — Shifting Sands, Community Care, 29.9-5.10.94.

Commission on Social Justice (1994) — Social Justice: Strategies for National Renewal - The Report of the Commission on Social Justice, London: Vintage.

Consumers' Association (1994) — Claiming Your Benefit, Which?, April.

Craig, G. (1990) — After the Fund was Over...?, Poverty, no. 77, Winter, 1990/1.

Crawford, R. and Meechan, G. (1992) — Welfare Rights and Community Care Assessment, Benefits, no.5, Sept./Oct.

Davies, C. (1988) — An Unsocial Suggestion, Community Care, 28.4.88.

Davis, A. (1984) — Help on the Hill, Social Work Today, vol. 15 no. 40, 18.6.84.

Davis, A. (1985) Confronting Poverty, Openmind, no. 12, Dec. 1984/Jan. 1985.

Davis, A. (1994) Maximum Benefits, Openmind, no. 70, Aug./Sept. 1994

Davis, A., Flynn, M. and Murray, J. (1993) Normal Lives?: The Financial Circumstances of People with Learning Disabilities, Manchester: National Development Team.

Deacon, A., Hylton, C., Karmani, A. and Law, I, (1994) Racial Equality and Social Security Delivery, Leeds: University of Leeds (School of Sociology and Social Policy).

Department of Health(1989) Caring for People: Community Care in the Next Decade and Beyond, Cm. 849, London: HMSO.

Department of Health (1994a) Community Care Special Transitional Grant 1995/96 - Distribution, consultation paper STG 95/3, London: DoH.

Department of Health(1994b) DiscretionaryCharges for Adult Social Services (Section 17 of the Health and Social Services and Social Security Adjudications Act 1983): Advice Note for Use by Social Services Inspectorate, Jan., London: DoH.

Department of Health(1994c) A Note on How Income from Charges Features in the Public Expenditure Process, memorandum to the Local Authority Associations, March, London: DoH.

Department of Health (1995) NHS Responsibilities for Meeting Continuing Health Care Needs, circular HSG(95)8/LAC(95)5, London: DoH.

Department of Health and Department of the Environment (1994) A Framework for Local Community Care Charters in England, London: DoH/DoE.

Department of Health and Social Security(1986) — Help with Board and Lodging Charges for People on Low Incomes: Proposals for Change, London: DHSS.

Department of Health and Welsh Office (1992) — Charging for Residential Accommodation Guide (loose leaf: periodically updated), London: DoH.

Department of Social Security (1988) — Help with Hostel Charges: Proposals for Change, London: DSS.

Department of Social Security (1993) — The Growth of Social Security, London: HMSO.

Department of Social Security (1994) — Income-Related Benefits: Estimates of Take-Up in 1990 and 1991, London: DSS.

Department of Social Security (1995) — Income-Related Benefits: Estimates of Take-Up in 1992, London: DSS.

Disability Alliance (1995) — Disability Rights Handbook (annually revised), London: Disability Alliance Educational and Research Association.

Divine, D. and Vaux, G. (1988) — Race and Poverty, in Becker, S. and MacPherson, S. (eds.), Public Issues, Private Pain: Poverty, Social Work and Social Policy, London: Social Services Insight Books.

Dix, G. and Huby, M. (1992) — Evaluating the Social Fund, London: HMSO.

European Commission (1994) — Germany: Compulsory State Insurance for the Nursing of Old or Handicapped People (Nursing - Insurance), MISSOC - Info: Bulletin of the Mutual Information System on Social Protection in the Community, no. 2/94.

Fimister, G. (1980) — Frontier Problems, in Coussins, J. (ed.), Dear SSAC: an Open Letter to the Social Security Advisory Committee, London: Child Poverty Action Group.

Fimister, G. (1986)   Welfare Rights Work in Social Services, London: British Association of Social Workers/ Macmillan.

Fimister, G. (1988)   Leaving Hospital After a Long Stay: the Role and Limitations of Social Security, in Baldwin, S.; Parker, G.; Walker, R. (eds.), Social Security and Community Care, Aldershot: Avebury.

Fimister, G. (1989)   A Piece of Sound Advice, Social Services Insight, vol. 4 no. 32, 6.12.89.

Fimister, G. (1990)   Wrong Incentive?, Social Services Insight, vol. 5 no. 20, 10.10.90.

Fimister, G. (1991)   Care in the Community: the Social Security Issues, in Carter, P.; Jeffs, T.; Smith, M.K. (eds.), Social Work and Social Welfare Yearbook 3, Milton Keynes: Open University Press.

Fimister, G. (1993a)   Community Care and the Benefits System, Benefits, no. 7, April/May.

Fimister, G. (1993b)   Benefit Regimes and Community Care, in Finding a Home for Community Care, London: Association of Metropolitan Authorities.

Fimister, G. (1993c)   Cash From Computers, Care Weekly, no. 302, 2.12.93.

Fimister, G. (1994)   Anti-Poverty Strategy: Origins and Options, discussion paper no. 1, London: Local Government Anti-Poverty Unit.

Fimister, G. (1995)   Social Justice?: Notes on the Social Security and Personal Taxation Aspects of the Final Report of the Commission on Social Justice, City of Newcastle upon Tyne: Welfare Rights Service.

Fimister, G. and Hill, M. (1993)

Delegating Implementation Problems: Social Security, Housing and Community Care in Britain, in Hill, M. (ed.), New Agendas in the Study of the Policy Process, Hemel Hempstead: Harvester Wheatsheaf.

Fimister, G. and Lister, R. (1981)

Social Security: the Case Against Contribution Tests, London: Child Poverty Action Group.

Firth, J. (Chair) (1987)

Public Support for Residential Care: Report of a Joint Central and Local Government Working Party, London: Dept. of Health and Social Security.

George, M. (1994a)

Paying Direct, Community Care, 25-31.8.94.

George, M. (1994b)

Adapt and Survive, Community Care, 6-12.10.94.

George, M. (1995)

Charged to Survive, Community Care, 6-11.1.95.

Glendinning, C. (1992)

The Costs of Informal Care: Looking Inside the Household, London: HMSO.

Godfrey, M. and Saxton, J. (1994)

Helping People with Mental Health Problems Claim Disability Living Allowance: a Practical Guide for Professionals and Other Advocates, Birmingham: University of Birmingham (Dept. of Social Policy and Social Work).

Griffiths, R. (1988)

Community Care: Agenda for Action, London: HMSO.

Griffiths, S. (1992) — Through Health Workers to Welfare Rights: a Report on the Health and Benefits Pilot in Goodinge and Finsbury Health Centres, Islington, 1991/92, London: Camden and Islington Family Health Services Authority/ London Borough of Islington.

Hadjipateras, A. and Witcher, S. (1991) — A Way Out of Poverty and Disability: Moving Towards a Comprehensive Disability Income Scheme, London: Disability Alliance.

Hancock, R. and Jarvis, C. (1994) — Long-Term Effects of Being a Carer: Main Findings from a Research Study, London: Age Concern Institute of Gerontology.

Harvey, A. and Robertson, G. (1995) — Survey of Charges for Social Care 1993-95, London: Local Government Anti-Poverty Unit.

Hayball, J. (1993) — Promoting Take-Up Amongst Home Care Clients, Benefits, no. 8, Sept./Oct.

Heywood, F. (1994) — Adaptations - Finding Ways to Say Yes, Bristol: University of Bristol(School for Advanced Urban Studies).

Hill, M. and Laing, P(1978) — Money Payments, Social Work and Supplementary Benefits: a Study of Section One of the 1963 Children and Young Persons Act, Bristol: University of Bristol (School for Advanced Urban Studies).

Hollander, D. and Weller, M. (1993) — Mentally Ill Suffer the Effects of Government Policy, letter, Guardian, 14.12.93.

House of Commons Health Committee (1993)

Community Care: the Way Forward, Vol. 1, Session 1992/3: Sixth Report, London: HMSO.

House of Commons Social Security Committee (1991)

The Financing of Private Residential and Nursing Home Fees, Session 1990/1: Fourth Report, London: HMSO

House of Commons Social Services Committee (1990a)

Community Care: Future Funding of Private and Voluntary Residential Care, Session 1989/90: Second Report, London : HMSO.

House of Commons Social Services Committee (1990b)

Community Care: Carers, Session 1989/90: Fifth Report, London: HMSO.

Ivory, M. (1994a)

Facilities Grant Cuts "Will Cause Hardship", news item, Community Care, 13.1.94.

Ivory, M. (1994b)

Welfare Rights Units Find Claims Shortfall, news item, Community Care, 2.7.92.

Laing, W. (1993)

Financing Long-Term Care: the Crucial Debate, London: Age Concern England.

Lakey, J. (1994)

Caring About Independence, London:Policy Studies Institute.

Land, H. (1988)

Social Security and Community Care: Creating "Perverse Incentives", in Baldwin, S.; Parker, G.; Walker, R. (eds.), Social Security and Community Care, Aldershot: Avebury.

Lilley, P. (1993)

Mais Lecture 1993 - Benefits and Costs: Securing the Future of Social Security, text of lecture, 23.6.93, London: Dept. of Social Security.

Lilley, P. (1995)   Speech by Rt. Hon. Peter Lilley MP, Secretary of State for Social Security, to the Social Market Foundation, 9 January 1995, text of speech, London: Dept. of Social Security.

Mc.Laughlin, E. (1992)   Mixed Blessings?: the Invalid Care Allowance and Carers' Income Needs, Benefits, no. 3, Jan./Feb.

Meen, G. (1994)   The Impact of Higher Rents, York: Joseph Rowntree Foundation.

Mitchell, D. (1993)   Charges Chop Elderly People's Spending Money, news item, Community Care, 10.6.93.

Nadash, P. and Zarb, G. (1994)   Cashing in on Independence: Comparing the Costs and Benefits of Cash and Services for Meeting Disabled Peoples' Support Needs, London: British Council of Organisations of Disabled People.

National Association of Citizens' Advice Bureaux (1991)   Beyond the Limit: Income Support for Elderly People in Residential Care and Nursing Homes, London: NACAB.

National Consumer Council (1977)   The Fourth Right of Citizenship: a Review of Local Advice Services, London: NCC.

National Health Service Executive (1994)   NHS Responsibilities for Meeting Long-Term Health Care Needs, Health Service Guidelines (draft), August, Leeds: NHS Executive.

National Welfare Rights Officers' Group (1991)   Care in the Community: the Role of Welfare Rights Officers - a Summary of Planning, Practice and Ethical Issues, London: National WROG (now the National Association of Welfare Rights Advisers).

Noble, M. and Smith, G. (1993)

Changing Benefits for Boarders and Hostel Dwellers: Unintended Consequences?, Benefits, no. 7, April/May.

Public Law Project (1994)

Challenging Community Care Decisions, London: Public Law Project.

Rainbow, H. (1993)

Income Maximisation in Community Care Assessment and in Continuing Care, Benefits, no. 7, April/May.

Scope (1995)

Disabled in Britain: Behind Closed Doors - The Carers' View, London: Scope.

Social Security Advisory Committee (1992)

The Social Fund: a New Structure, London: HMSO.

Supplementary Benefits Commission (1977)

Discretionary Payments to the Unemployed in the Nineteen-Thirties, in Report of the Supplementary Benefits Commission for the Year Ended 31 December 1976, Cm. 6910, London: HMSO.

Thomas, D. (1993)

Access Denied, Law Society Gazette, Dec.

Titmuss, R. (1963)

Commitment to Welfare, London: Allen and Unwin.

Vaux, G. (1994)

The Underpayment of Social Security Benefits, Consumer Policy Review, vol. 4 no. 3, July.

Wagner, Lady (Chair) (1988)

Residential Care: a Positive Choice -Report of the Independent Review of Residential Care, London: HMSO/ National Institute of Social Work.

Wilcox, S. (1994)

The Costs of Higher Rents, in Housing Finance Review 1994/95, York: Joseph Rowntree Foundation.

Wright, C. (1994) Brain Injury Patient "Was Discharged to Free Bed", news item, Daily Telegraph, 3.2.94.

Young, P. (1988) The Provision of Care in Supported Lodgings and Unregistered Homes, London: Office of Population Censuses and Surveys.

Appendix 1:

List of Abbreviations

AA	Attendance Allowance
ACC	Association of County Councils
ADSS	Association of Directors of Social Services
AIDS	Acquired Immuno-Deficiency Syndrome
AMA	Association of Metropolitan Authorities
BA	Benefits Agency (the operational arm of the DSS)
BMA	British Medical Association
CAB	Citizens' Advice Bureau
CPAG	Child Poverty Action Group
CTB	Council Tax Benefit
DHSS	Department of Health and Social Security (since 1988, divided into DoH and DSS)
DLA	Disability Living Allowance
DLAC	Disability Living Allowance (care component)
DLAM	Disability Living Allowance (mobility component)
DoE	Department of the Environment
DoH	Department of Health

DSS	Department of Social Security
GP	General Practitioner
HASSASSA	Health and Social Services and Social Security Adjudications Act 1983
HB	Housing Benefit
HIV	Human Immuno-Deficiency Virus
HMSO	Her Majesty's Stationery Office
ILF	Independent Living Fund
IS	Income Support
LA	Local Authority
MA	Mobility Allowance (replaced by DLAM in 1992)
MP	Member of Parliament
NCC	National Consumer Council
NHS	National Health Service
PEA	Personal Expenses Allowance
P&V	Private and Voluntary
RP	Retirement Pension
SDA	Severe Disablement Allowance

SSAC   Social Security Advisory Committee

SSD   Social Services Department (see chapter 1, para. 1, re. Scottish Social Work Departments)

STG   Special Transitional Grant

UK   United Kingdom

Appendix 2:

Chronology of Key Events (1980+)

This list is designed to help the reader locate in time some of the key events from 1980 to the mid-1990s.

1980:

Supplementary benefit (the means-tested social assistance benefit which was the predecessor of income support) had hitherto been based on wide-ranging discretion, albeit hedged about with voluminous administrative guidance. From 1980, it was placed on a different footing, with the introduction of a mass of detailed regulations. Largely designed to achieve spending restraint, the changes had the side-effect of making some payments easier to claim, including benefit in respect of care home charges.

1983:

Restrictions on supplementary benefit payable in respect of care home charges were tightened up, with a new system of local limits.

1985:

Restrictions on supplementary benefit for care home charges were more severely tightened, with the introduction of national limits.

1988:

In April, there were major changes to the structure of means-tested benefits, including the replacement of supplementary benefit by income support and of "single payments" (grants) by the Social Fund (dealing mainly in loans).

1988:

Publication of the Griffiths Report, proposing substantial reorganisation of the allocation of resources and responsibilities in relation to care services.

1988:

Department of Health and Social Security split into two separate departments.

1989:

Special income support rules for boarders withdrawn in April.

1989:

Special income support rules for hostel-dwellers withdrawn in October.

1989:

Publication of Caring for People, the community care White Paper, which accepted most of the Griffiths proposals.

1990:

NHS and Community Care Act: established the framework of the new community care arrangements.

1991:

April was the original target date for the implementation of the new arrangements. They were, in the event, deferred for two years.

1992:

Attendance allowance and mobility allowance restructured as disability living allowance (care and mobility components) (attendance allowance being retained for certain older claimants - see chapter 3).

1993:

In April, the new community care arrangements were introduced, whereby local authority SSDs acquired lead responsibility for the finance and organisation of services.

1993:

In April, the requirement for private or voluntary sector care homes to register with the health or social services registration authority was extended to "small homes" (those with less than four residents) if they provide both board and personal care. At the same time, registration became the determining factor as to whether a resident falls under the "more dependent" or "less dependent" benefit regime. A similar distinction was incorporated into the charging rules (but with some flexibility - see chapter 5).

1995:

In March, the DoH published its guidance on NHS Responsibilities for Meeting Continuing Health Care Needs, in response to considerable controversy over allegations of "dumping" of patients onto SSDs.

1995:

In April, incapacity benefit replaced invalidity (and sickness) benefit. More severe eligibility criteria are intended considerably to reduce the number of beneficiaries.

1995:

In October, cuts in housing benefit affecting new claims in the deregulated private rented sector (and a number of housing association places) are scheduled to be introduced (see chapters 3, 4 and 7).

1996:

In October, the jobseeker's allowance is scheduled to replace unemployment benefit (and income support for unemployed people). As in the case of incapacity benefit, the eligibility criteria will be designed to cut the numbers entitled. For community care service users who are able to enter the labour market, aggressive administration may be a problem.

Appendix 3:

Glossary of Terms

Given the rich variety of jargon within the community care, local government and social security fields, a note of the sense in which various terms are used in this book may be of help to readers.

Please note that this list does not include specific benefits: the key benefits in the community care context are described briefly in chapter 3.

CARE IN THE COMMUNITY: This expression is used to describe the broad approach which seeks to support service users as independently as possible in their own homes or in other relatively independent settings (such as group homes or supported lodgings). The term is sometimes also used, where the context so requires, to embrace residential and nursing home care, as it is with the finance of these that policy in relation to "care in the community" is often substantially concerned.

CASE LAW: Interpretation of the law by the higher courts and Social Security Commissioners. Their decisions are binding precedents in respect of similar future cases. (The Government has tried to restrict their retrospective effect in the social security field).

COMMUNITY CARE: The term is used interchangeably with "care in the community" (see above). No subtle distinction between the two expressions is intended.

CONTRIBUTORY BENEFITS: Those which derive from formulae relating to contributions paid (or deemed to have been paid) into the national insurance system over specified time periods (which vary between benefits).

COUPLES: Used in this book to refer to heterosexual couples, either married or unmarried. Homosexual couples of either sex are treated as separate individuals throughout the benefit system. As regards charging, all couples should be assessed as separate individuals. In the residential care context, powers to pursue "liable relatives" for a contribution to the charge apply only to married couples. The DoH's view, put forward in the context of non-residential care, that a service user might have "sufficiently reliable access" to resources not held in his or her own name to merit taking them into account (see chapter 5) could presumably apply in theory not only to heterosexual but also to homosexual couples. However, this latter line seems potentially controversial and unlikely to be pursued in practice.

DAY CARE: Care services provided on a non-residential basis, but away from the service user's own home.

DOMICILIARY CARE/DOMICILIARY SERVICES: Care services provided in the service user's own home.

GROUP HOMES: Accommodation for small groups of people, typically with learning difficulties or mental illness, who are able to enjoy a greater degree of independence than would be the case in a residential care setting. Normally provided in ordinary rented housing.

HOSTELS: Used in this book to describe shared accommodation which involves general support and/or counselling and/ or personal care, usually entailing a lower level of dependence on such services than would apply in a residential care home. The range is in fact considerable, from relatively general practical support - where the problem addressed by the project is essentially, say, homelessness or domestic violence - to substantial personal care at the other end of the continuum. The term is not intended to be construed in any technical sense derived from social security or housing legislation, unless the context so requires. (For the precise definition used by the DSS in its 1987-8 review of income support for hostel-dwellers, see chapter 2).

INCOME SUPPORT: The term is not used in this book in a general sense, but rather to refer to the specific benefit of that name (see chapter 3 for a brief description).

LOCAL AUTHORITY ASSOCIATIONS: Organisations which represent the collective interests of LAs in dealings with central government. In Great Britain, the main such bodies are the Association of County Councils (ACC); the Association of District Councils (ADC); the Association of Metropolitan Authorities(AMA); and the Convention of Scottish Local Authorities (CoSLA).At the time of writing, the ACC, ADC and AMA are considering a merger.

MEANS-TESTED BENEFITS: Those where entitlement depends upon the outcome of a test of financial resources.

NATIONAL INSURANCE: See "contributory benefits" above.

OCCUPATIONAL PENSIONS: Those paid by schemes operated by an employer rather than by the state.

PARTNER: A member of a married or unmarried couple. (See "couples", above).

PERSONAL EXPENSES ALLOWANCE: The amount of income left to a care home resident after paying the SSD's charge for the place in the home.

PRIVATE PENSIONS: Those paid by schemes operated by private sector financial institutions. (Not used in this book to include occupational pensions - see above).

RESIDENTIAL CARE: Care provided in a residential care home. Sometimes, depending on the context, may also embrace nursing home care. Not used in this book to describe accommodation associated with more "independent living", such as supported lodgings, even where these are registered with the SSD as care homes.

RESPITE CARE: A term which usually describes temporary residential care designed to give a carer a break from his or her caring responsibilities. (While in general use at the time of writing, I have heard it suggested that the term is becoming stigmatised, as having negative overtones in respect of the cared-for person).

REVENUE SUPPORT GRANT: The main vehicle whereby central government supports LA spending.

SOCIAL ASSISTANCE: Term used to refer to means-tested schemes which top up incomes to a basic level. In the UK, this is the income support scheme (supplementary benefit prior to April 1988).

SOCIAL INSURANCE: Called "national insurance" in the UK. See "contributory benefits", above.

SOCIAL SECURITY: Used in this book in the wide sense of both means-tested and non-means-tested benefits (rather than the narrower sense of contributory benefits only).

SOCIAL SECURITY APPEAL TRIBUNALS: Local tribunals which hear appeals against the decisions of social security adjudication officers. (Appeals concerning disability questions relating to AA, DLA or disability working allowance are heard by Disability Appeal Tribunals instead).

SOCIAL SECURITY COMMISSIONERS: Legal adjudicators who hear further appeals on points of law against the decisions of local Social Security Appeal Tribunals (and Disability Appeal Tribunals). They have the same status as High Court judges and their decisions constitute case law. (See "Social Security Appeal Tribunals" and "case law" above).

SUPPORTED ACCOMMODATION: Used in this book in a broad sense to indicate accommodation where some degree of personal care and/or general support and/or counselling is provided to residents. Ranges from residential care and nursing homes to hostels and board and lodging situations where support is provided.

SUPPORTED LODGINGS: More specific than "supported accommodation" (see above). Refers to small-scale board and lodging situations.

TENANT: Used in the broad sense to include licensees.

Index

Notes to Index

*(1) Some subjects (for example, supported accommodation of one sort and another; domiciliary care; resettlement from long-stay institutions; references to "client groups" and associated disabilities) arise very frequently throughout the book and therefore do not lend themselves to detailed indexing. The same applies to certain key agencies (Social Services Departments; local authorities; the Benefits Agency).

*(2) Some substantial subjects (for example, finance of services; charging for services; advice and advocacy) are indexed by reference to the chapter in which the most detailed discussion of that subject is to be found.